Exploring Italy's Hidden Gems a Unique Guide to Uncharted Monuments, Places, Food and Wines

JULIO DE CESARI

Copyright © 2023 Julio De Cesari

All rights reserved.

ISBN: 9798871713105

DEDICATION

To you, the Explorer of heart and soul, who finds magic in the roads less traveled and joy in discoveries not marked on maps. This journey through Italy's lesser-known is dedicated to you, in the hope that each page brings you closer to the hidden beauty and untold stories. May you find in its words not just an itinerary, but an invitation to live, love and dream.

With affection, Julio De Cesari

Exploring Italy's Hidden Gems: A Unique Guide to Uncharted Monuments, Places, Food and Wines

Chapter 1: Introduction to Italy's Hidden Gems

1.1 Author's Preface

1.2 The Importance of Exploring Lesser-Known Destinations

1.3 Unveiling Italy's Hidden Gems

1.4 How to Discover Off-the-Beaten-Path Places

1.5 Planning Your Itinerary: Tips and Suggestions

1.6 Understanding the Cultural Significance of Lesser-Known Treasures

1.7 Sustainable Tourism and Preserving Italy's Hidden Gems

1.8 Overcoming Language Barriers and Navigating Local Customs

1.9 Recommendations for Immersive Travel Experiences

Chapter 2: Northern Italy's Hidden Gems

2.1 Delights of Valle d'Aosta

2.2 Unveiling the Charms of Piedmont

2.3 Exploring the Enchanting Lakes of Lombardy

2.4 Discovering the Beauty of Liguria

2.5 Unforgettable Experiences in Emilia-Romagna

2.6 Hidden Cultural Gems of Trentino-Alto Adige

2.7 Discover the Hidden

2.8 Off-the-Beaten-Path in Friuli-Venezia Giulia

Chapter 3: Central Italy's Hidden Gems

3.1 Uncovering the Secrets of Tuscany

3.2 Discover the Hidden Gems of Umbria, the 'Green Heart of Italy

3.3 Exploring the Authenticity of Marche

3.4 Off-the-Beaten-Path in Lazio

3.5 Delights of the Vatican City and Rome

3.6 Lesser-Known Wonders of Abruzzo

Chapter 4: Southern Italy's Hidden Gems

4.1 Lesser-Known Wonders of Sardinia

4.2 Discovering the Charm of Campania

4.3 Hidden Cultural Gems of Molise

4.4 Unveiling the Mysteries of Puglia

4.5 Exploring the Authenticity of Basilicata

4.6 Hidden Gems of Calabria

4.7 Off-the-Beaten-Path in Sicily

4.8 Delights of the Southern Italian Islands

Chapter 5: Hidden Gems of Italy's Islands

5.1 Hidden Gems of the Tuscan Archipelago

5.2 Exploring the Authenticity of the Pontine Islands

5.3 Off-the-Beaten-Path in the Maddalena Archipelago

5.4 Delights of the Tremiti Islands

5.5 Lesser-Known Wonders of the Egadi Islands

5.6 Secrets of the Aeolian Islands

5.7 Hidden Cultural Gems of the Pelagie Islands

Chapter 6: Unique Italian Experiences

6.1 Wine and Gastronomy Adventures

6.2 Unconventional Beach Escapes

6.3 Hiking and Nature Trails

6.4 Historical and Architectural Marvels

6.5 Art and Culture Immersion

6.6 Enchanting Rural Villages

6.7 Hidden Gems for Adventure Seekers

6.8 Unveiling Italy's Underground Treasures

Chapter 7: Off-the-Beaten-Path Experiences

7.1 Immersing in Local Festivals and Traditions

7.2 Exploring Italy's Hidden Natural Wonders

7.3 Uncovering Italy's Lesser-Known Archaeological Sites

7.4 Delving into Italy's Artistic Hidden Gems

7.5 Discovering Hidden Culinary Delights

7.6 Off-the-Beaten-Path Hiking Trails

7.7 Exploring Italy's Hidden Beaches

7.8 Unique Shopping Experiences: Local Artisans and Boutiques

Chapter 8: Practical Tips and Recommendations

8.1 Transportation Options: Getting Around in Italy

8.2 Accommodation: Choosing Unique and Authentic Stays

8.3 Dining Tips: Trying Local Cuisine

8.4 Language Essentials: Useful Phrases and Expressions

8.5 Safety Considerations for Off-the-Beaten-Path Travel

Chapter 9: Conclusion

9.1 Reflecting on the Hidden Gems Explored

9.2 Inspiring Future Adventures

9.3 Leaving a Positive Impact

9.4 Final Thoughts

9.5 Copyright

ACKNOWLEDGMENTS

In the journey of bringing "Exploring Italy's Hidden Gems" to life, I have been fortunate to have the support and encouragement of many. This book, a tapestry of Italy's lesser-known wonders, would not have been possible without the collective contribution of these remarkable individuals.

Firstly, I extend my deepest gratitude to my family, whose love and understanding have been the bedrock of my endeavors. Your belief in my vision has been a constant source of strength.

To my friends, who shared in my travels and discoveries, offering insights and laughter along the way – your companionship made every hidden alley and sunlit piazza all the more memorable.

I owe a debt of gratitude to the local experts, historians, and everyday citizens of Italy who generously shared their knowledge and stories, breathing life into every page with their authentic experiences and perspectives.

A special thanks to the team of editors and designers whose meticulous attention to detail and creative brilliance have given shape to my words and visions. Your dedication has been instrumental in transforming a collection of stories and advice into a guide that will, I hope, inspire many.

I am also grateful to the various communities and organizations across Italy that welcomed me with open arms, allowing me to delve deep into the heart of local life and culture.

Lastly, I thank you, the reader, for embarking on this journey with me. Your curiosity and passion for exploration are the ultimate inspiration for works like this. May this book serve as your compass to the extraordinary, yet often overlooked, corners of Italy.

With heartfelt thanks, Julio De Cesari

Chapter 1: Introduction to Italy's Hidden Gems

1.1 Author's Preface

Dear Explorer,

Welcome to a journey unlike any other, one that weaves together the allure of Italy's famed cities with the hidden splendor of its lesser-known treasures. "Exploring Italy's Hidden Gems: Unveiling the Lesser-Known Treasures," authored by Julio De Cesari, is a testament to a lifetime of exploration, crafted with the inquisitive foreign tourist in mind.

While the grandeur of Rome, Florence, Venice, Naples, and Milan has captured hearts worldwide, this guide takes you on a different path. It's an anthology that delves deep into the Italy that simmers quietly in the shadows of these renowned giants - a land of uncharted beauty waiting to be discovered.

Through my years of traversing Italy, from its sun-kissed coasts to the shadowed alleys of ancient towns, I've uncovered hidden treasures, far removed from the typical tourist's path. This journey is not about the well-trodden streets immortalized in photographs and documentaries. Instead, it celebrates those secret corners of Italy where the essence of Italian life thrives, vibrant and untouched by mainstream tourism's glare.

This book is more than a guide; it's a narrative rich in history, art, landscape, and cuisine, narrated by someone who has not just seen but lived the true Italian experience. You will find not an exhaustive encyclopedia of Italy's wonders, but a carefully curated collection of lesser-known jewels. These are the places where Italy's heart beats strongest, away from the dazzling spotlight that shines on its more famous cities.

"Exploring Italy's Hidden Gems" invites you to step off the beaten path and embrace Italy in its purest form. It's an invitation to discover an Italy that's not just seen, but felt; an Italy that remains with you long after you've returned home. This guide is a call to the adventurous soul, eager to uncover the well-kept secrets of a land rich in history and culture, and to those seeking an authentic experience, far from the crowded tourist spots.

So, dear traveler, join me, Julio De Cesari, on this extraordinary journey. Let us leave behind the familiar and dive into the heart of Italy's true magnificence. Here's to the hidden gems that make Italy an endless adventure for the soul, to places that don't just charm you, but captivate your heart forever.

Yours in exploration,

Julio De Cesari

1.2 The Importance of Exploring Lesser-Known Destinations

Imagine a journey that takes you beyond the bustling streets of Italy's famous cities, a journey that unveils the hidden heart of this enchanting country. While the grandeur of Rome, the artistic legacy of Florence, and the romantic canals of Venice are the usual highlights, Italy's true essence often lies hidden in its less-traveled paths. These hidden gems offer a gateway to an Italy less known but equally mesmerizing, rich with undiscovered culture, history, and natural beauty. Let's embark on a captivating voyage to explore the quaint towns, serene islands, and artistic havens that represent Italy's diverse and vibrant soul.

Travel enthusiasts often gravitate towards famed Italian cities like Rome, Florence, and Venice, drawn by their iconic attractions and historical allure. However, beyond these popular destinations lies a treasure trove of hidden Italian gems, each offering a distinct and authentic experience far from the tourist throngs.

Italy's less frequented locales invite travelers to a world brimming with rich culture, intriguing history, and breathtaking natural beauty. These under-the-radar spots promise more intimate encounters, allowing deeper connections with local life and the country's diverse landscapes and regional peculiarities.

Consider the mesmerizing town of Matera in Basilicata, a jewel nestled in Italy's southern terrain. This ancient city, etched into the rocky cliffs, marries history with unique architecture. The "Sassi" – ancient cave dwellings now repurposed into boutique accommodations, eateries, and shops – offer an enchanting exploration. Matera, a UNESCO World Heritage Site and a cinematic backdrop for films like "The Passion of the Christ," captivates with its haunting beauty and timeless charm.

Art and culture aficionados should not miss Urbino in the Marche region, the birthplace of Renaissance maestro Raphael. Urbino is a haven of artistic legacy, where cobblestone streets wind through a labyrinth of historic edifices. The majestic Palazzo Ducale, home to the National Gallery of the Marche, stands as a testament to the town's artistic grandeur. Delve into the vibrant local art scene, visit Raphael's home, and venture into the countryside to behold the undulating hills of the Marche landscape.

For a serene getaway, the Aeolian Islands off Sicily's coast are a perfect choice. This volcanic archipelago, comprising seven distinct islands, offers a slice of paradise for those seeking natural splendor. From Stromboli's imposing cliffs to Salina's unspoiled beaches, these islands are a sanctuary for nature enthusiasts. Embark on boat excursions to discover secluded coves, hike volcanic trails for stunning vistas, and bask in the tranquility of the Mediterranean's embrace.

Exploring these lesser-known Italian destinations not only provides a refreshing escape from bustling tourist centers but also an opportunity to immerse in Italy's authentic charm. These locations offer a chance to engage with the local populace, embrace regional lifestyles, and uncover Italy's hidden corners. Whether you're in search of adventure or a peaceful retreat, Italy's lesser-known gems await to enrich your travel diary with enduring memories and a profound appreciation of the nation's diverse cultural tapestry.

1.3 Unveiling Italy's Hidden Gems

Italy, a country celebrated for its iconic cities like Rome, Venice, and Florence, also harbors a wealth of lesser-known marvels. These hidden gems, scattered across the Italian landscape, are ripe for discovery by those seeking a more authentic and diverse travel experience.

Every region of Italy boasts its own secret wonders. From the breathtaking coastal towns of Cinque Terre in Liguria to the quaint charm of the Amalfi Coast in Campania, Italy's lesser-trodden paths are as diverse as they are captivating. These destinations offer a genuine taste of Italian life, far removed from the bustling tourist centers.

Cinque Terre, a series of five vibrant fishing villages perched along the Italian Riviera, is a spectacle of color and natural beauty. Hiking trails weave through the cliffs, linking the towns and unveiling secluded coves and culinary delights. The local cuisine, rich in fresh seafood and regional flavors, is a journey in itself.

In contrast, the Amalfi Coast in Campania is a stretch of coastline renowned for its dramatic cliffside villages, lush lemon groves, and luxurious ambiance. Strolling through these villages, you encounter historical architecture, artisanal shops, and the alluring scent of authentic limoncello.

Venturing into Basilicata, the town of Matera awaits with its labyrinth of ancient sassi – cave dwellings that have stood the test of time. This UNESCO World Heritage site offers a unique blend of history and culture, where modern life intertwines with ancient structures.

Meanwhile, in Sicily, the majestic ruins of Agrigento's Valley of the Temples stand as a testament to the grandeur of ancient Greek civilization. These well-preserved temples, dating back to the 5th century BC, offer a window into a bygone era of architectural brilliance.

The Italian Riviera in Liguria and the picturesque countryside of Umbria add to Italy's mosaic of hidden spots. The Riviera, with its captivating landscapes and quaint coastal towns, and Umbria's rolling hills and medieval villages, both present a serene escape from the typical tourist itinerary.

In conclusion, Italy's array of hidden gems provides an immersive and diverse travel experience. From the vibrant vistas of Cinque Terre and the historical depth of Matera and Agrigento to the serene beauty of the Amalfi Coast, these lesser-known destinations invite travelers to explore the multifaceted charm and rich heritage of Italy. Embarking on this journey off the beaten path promises not only breathtaking scenery and cultural richness but also an authentic encounter with the heart and soul of Italy.

1.4 How to Discover Off-the-Beaten-Path Places

When it comes to discovering off-the-beaten-path places in Italy, there are a few strategies that can help you uncover hidden gems that most tourists overlook. Here are some tips to guide you in your quest for unique and lesser-known destinations: 1. Research and Plan Ahead: Before embarking on your trip, spend some time researching the less popular regions and towns in Italy. Look for travel blogs, forums, and local recommendations to get an idea of the places that are off the radar of mainstream tourism. Make a list of the places that intrigue you and start planning your itinerary accordingly. 2. Embrace Slow Travel: Instead of rushing from one famous attraction to another, slow down and allow yourself to explore the lesser-known towns and villages. This will give you a chance to experience the authentic local culture and interact with the friendly residents. By embracing slow travel, you might stumble upon hidden treasures that are not mentioned in guidebooks. 3. Get Off the Main Roads: To discover Italy's hidden gems, you need to venture off the main roads and explore the countryside. Rent a car or take local transportation to reach the remote and secluded places. Be open to taking detours and following the winding paths that lead to charming villages, picturesque landscapes, and untouched natural wonders. 4. Connect with Locals: One of the best ways to uncover the lesser-known treasures of Italy is by connecting with the locals. Strike up conversations with the residents, visit local markets, cafes, and restaurants, and ask for their recommendations. The locals will often share their favorite hidden spots that are not frequented by tourists, giving you an authentic and unique experience. 5. Seek Out Cultural Festivals and Events: Italy is known for its vibrant festivals and events that celebrate its rich history, traditions, and local culture. Keep an eye out for lesser-known festivals happening in the regions you plan to visit. Attending these events will not only expose you to the local traditions but also introduce you to hidden gems that come alive during these special occasions. 6. Explore the Islands: Italy boasts a plethora of enchanting islands, many of which are lesser-known compared to popular destinations like Capri or Sicily. Consider visiting islands such as Procida, Pantelleria, or the Aeolian Islands. These hidden gems offer pristine beaches, charming villages, and a tranquil atmosphere that will make your trip truly memorable. By following these strategies, you can unlock the secrets of Italy's hidden gems and create a travel experience that goes beyond the well-trodden tourist paths. Embrace the unknown, be open to serendipitous discoveries, and let the beauty of Italy's lesser-known treasures enchant you.

1.5 Planning Your Itinerary: Tips and Suggestions

When planning your itinerary for exploring Italy's hidden gems, there are a few tips and suggestions to keep in mind. Whether you have a limited amount of time or are looking to cover multiple regions, these considerations will help you make the most of your trip:

1. Prioritize Your Interests: Italy offers a plethora of attractions, from historic sites to breathtaking landscapes and delicious cuisine. Before finalizing your itinerary, think about what interests you the most. Are you a history enthusiast? Do you prefer exploring nature? Or are you a food lover? By prioritizing your interests, you can tailor your itinerary to include the hidden gems that align with your passions.

2. Research and Discover Hidden Gems: While popular destinations like Rome, Florence, and Venice are undoubtedly stunning, don't forget to delve deeper into Italy's lesser-known treasures. Research and uncover hidden gems that are off the beaten path. Whether it's a charming coastal town, a quaint countryside village, or a lesser-explored region, these hidden gems often offer a more authentic and unique experience.

3. Consider the Time of Year: Italy experiences different tourist seasons throughout the year. If you prefer quieter surroundings and cheaper accommodations, consider visiting during the shoulder or off-peak seasons. Spring (April to June) and autumn (September to October) are generally less crowded, offering you a chance to explore hidden gems without the bustling crowds.

4. Plan for Sufficient Time in Each Destination: While it can be tempting to cover multiple regions in a short period, rushing through each destination

may leave you feeling exhausted and unsatisfied. Instead, allocate sufficient time in each place to truly immerse yourself in its charm. This will allow you to fully appreciate the hidden gems you discover and create lasting memories.

5. Embrace Local Experiences: One of the best ways to uncover Italy's hidden gems is by embracing local experiences. Interact with the locals, try regional dishes, participate in cultural events, and explore local markets. Engaging with the local community will not only enrich your trip but may also lead you to hidden gems that are not commonly found in travel guides.

6. Be Flexible and Open to Unexpected Discoveries: While it's important to have a well-planned itinerary, leave room for spontaneity and unexpected discoveries. Sometimes the most memorable experiences come from stumbling upon hidden gems that were not on your original list. Embrace the unknown and be open to exploring off-the-beaten-path destinations that capture your curiosity.

By keeping these considerations in mind, you can create an itinerary that allows you to uncover and appreciate Italy's hidden gems to the fullest. Remember, the joy of travel lies in the journey itself, so embrace every moment and immerse yourself in the beauty and charm that Italy has to offer.

1.6 Understanding the Cultural Significance of Lesser-Known Treasures

While Italy's famed cities like Rome, Florence, and Venice are celebrated globally for their historical and artistic splendor, the country's lesser-known locales are where the depth of its cultural tapestry truly unravels. These hidden gems, often overshadowed by popular tourist destinations, harbor untold stories and traditions integral to understanding Italy's diverse heritage. Delving into these places allows travelers to connect deeply with the nation's history, engage with local communities, and participate in authentic cultural practices, all while contributing to sustainable tourism.

Matera in Basilicata, with its ancient "Sassi" cave dwellings, is a testament to human resilience and ingenuity. This UNESCO World Heritage Site, dating back millennia, offers a tangible connection to past lives and traditions. Exploring Matera is not just a journey through its winding alleys and stone houses; it's an exploration of the enduring human spirit that characterizes

Italian culture.

In contrast, Bologna, often overlooked in favor of more famous cities, is a hub of gastronomic, architectural, and academic wealth. Home to the world's oldest university, it stands as a beacon of intellectual heritage. Wandering through Bologna's historic streets, visitors can immerse themselves in a vibrant blend of culinary delights, medieval architecture, and a thriving cultural scene that echoes the scholarly pursuits of centuries.

The Cinque Terre, a string of five fishing villages on the Italian Riviera, exemplifies Italy's coastal charm. Each village, with its unique allure, showcases traditional fishing culture, terraced vineyards, and a slower pace of life. Here, one can experience the quintessence of Italian coastal living, from the fresh seafood to the stunning Mediterranean vistas, all while walking through the vibrant, narrow streets that echo with stories of the past.

Venturing into these less explored regions not only offers a window into Italy's rich cultural landscape but also supports sustainable tourism practices. Engaging with local communities in these areas fosters meaningful cultural exchange and helps preserve the authenticity and traditions of these places.

In essence, to fully embrace Italy's historical and artistic legacy, one must explore beyond its famed landmarks. The hidden gems scattered across the country, from Matera's ancient caves to Bologna's intellectual richness and the serene beauty of Cinque Terre, are crucial to understanding the mosaic of Italian culture. They offer a more nuanced and immersive experience, allowing travelers to uncover the true essence of Italy and its diverse cultural fabric.

1.7 Sustainable Tourism and Preserving Italy's Hidden Gems

Sustainable tourism plays a crucial role in preserving Italy's hidden gems and ensuring their long-term sustainability. As travelers continue to gravitate towards off-the-beaten-path destinations, it becomes increasingly important to strike a balance between tourism and conservation. One of the key aspects of sustainable tourism is minimizing the negative environmental impacts caused by excessive visitor numbers. This can be achieved through responsible travel practices such as reducing carbon footprints, conserving water and energy, and supporting local businesses that prioritize eco-friendly initiatives. Additionally, sustainable tourism encourages tourists to engage in activities that promote cultural preservation and respect for local traditions. By immersing themselves in the local customs, cuisine, and arts, travelers contribute to the preservation of Italy's rich cultural heritage. Furthermore, sustainable tourism fosters a deeper connection between visitors and the lesser-known destinations, allowing them to appreciate the unique beauty and historical significance of these hidden gems. It also creates opportunities for local communities to benefit economically from tourism while maintaining their cultural identity. By embracing sustainable tourism practices, we can ensure that Italy's hidden gems remain treasures for generations to come.

To achieve this, responsible travel practices are essential. Travelers can reduce their carbon footprints by opting for eco-friendly transportation options such as public transit or bicycles. Additionally, conserving water and energy while staying in accommodations can greatly contribute to minimizing environmental harm. Supporting local businesses that prioritize eco-friendly initiatives also plays a significant role in sustainable tourism. By purchasing locally-made products and dining at restaurants that source ingredients from nearby farms, travelers can support the local economy and reduce the environmental impact of their visit.

However, sustainable tourism goes beyond just environmental considerations. It also encourages tourists to engage in activities that promote cultural preservation and respect for local traditions. By immersing themselves in the local customs, cuisine, and arts, travelers become active participants in the preservation of Italy's rich cultural heritage. They can attend traditional festivals, visit local artisans' workshops, or even take part in cooking classes to learn about and appreciate the local traditions.

Furthermore, sustainable tourism fosters a deeper connection between visitors and the lesser-known destinations, allowing them to appreciate the unique beauty and historical significance of these hidden gems. By exploring off-the-beaten-path locations, travelers can discover the charm of lesser-known towns, villages, and natural landscapes. This not only enriches their travel experience but also contributes to the preservation of these hidden gems by bringing attention and appreciation to them.

Moreover, sustainable tourism creates opportunities for local communities to benefit economically from tourism while maintaining their cultural identity. By engaging with local businesses, travelers can support sustainable livelihoods and contribute to the economic growth of these communities. This, in turn, helps to maintain the authenticity and charm of the destinations, as the local communities are able to preserve their traditions and way of life.

1.8 Overcoming Language Barriers and Navigating Local Customs

Traveling to Italy, with its rich cultural heritage and diverse linguistic landscape, calls for preparation to navigate language barriers and cultural nuances. While English is widely spoken in major cities and tourist spots, venturing into smaller towns and rural areas may present language challenges. To enhance your travel experience and connect with locals, learning basic Italian phrases is invaluable. Simple greetings like 'ciao' (hello), 'grazie' (thank you), and essential questions can bridge communication gaps and foster goodwill.

Carrying a phrasebook or utilizing translation apps on your smartphone can be a lifeline in various scenarios, from deciphering menus to asking for directions. Familiarizing yourself with these tools beforehand allows for smoother interactions and a deeper immersion in Italian life. Remember, while technology is helpful, a personal effort to speak even a few words in Italian is often more appreciated by locals.

Beyond language, understanding and respecting Italian customs and traditions is crucial. Italians place a high value on politeness, so common courtesies like greeting with 'buongiorno' (good morning) or 'buonasera' (good evening) and a smile make a significant impact. Familiarize yourself with local customs, including dining etiquette, appropriate dress codes, and social norms. For instance, learning the basics of Italian table manners, such as the proper way to eat pasta and the placement of bread on the table, not only shows respect but also enriches your culinary experiences.

Adapting to Italian dining customs, where meals are often leisurely and social, will also enhance your enjoyment of Italy's famed culinary delights. Understanding that meals are more than just eating but an opportunity for conversation and connection can transform your dining experiences into memorable cultural exchanges.

By equipping yourself with basic Italian phrases and an understanding of local customs, you'll navigate Italy with greater confidence and enjoyment. Embracing the Italian language and culture not only facilitates smoother communication but also demonstrates respect and appreciation for the rich traditions of this beautiful country. So, before embarking on your Italian journey, invest some time in learning key phrases and familiarizing yourself with Italian customs. Your efforts will enrich your travel experience and lead to more meaningful interactions with the locals.

1.9 Recommendations for Immersive Travel Experiences

Italy, a land steeped in history, art, and culinary excellence, offers far more than just its well-known landmarks and bustling cities. For the discerning traveler looking to delve deeper into the authentic Italian experience, there are countless opportunities to explore and engage with the country's rich cultural fabric. From savoring traditional cuisine to participating in local festivities and uncovering historical wonders, Italy is a treasure trove of hidden gems waiting to be discovered. Let's explore some key recommendations that promise to enrich your journey and provide a truly immersive Italian experience:

1.Culinary Delights: Italian cuisine is a window into the country's culture. Enroll in a cooking class to learn the art of making authentic pasta, pizza, or gelato. This hands-on experience offers more than just culinary skills; it's an insight into Italy's gastronomic traditions and family recipes handed down through generations.

2.Local Festivals and Celebrations: Dive into Italy's festive spirit by attending local events. Join the vibrant Carnevale in Venice, experience the historic Palio in Siena, or celebrate Festa della Repubblica in Rome. These festivals are a mosaic of music, dance, and traditional customs, showcasing Italy's rich cultural tapestry.

3.Art and History Tours: Italy's artistic and historical wealth is unparalleled. Embark on guided tours of landmarks like Rome's Colosseum, Florence's Uffizi Gallery, or the Vatican Museums. Expert guides will enhance your appreciation of the art, architecture, and stories behind these iconic sites.

4.Rural Retreats: For a tranquil experience, retreat to Italy's countryside. Agriturismos offer a genuine taste of rural life. Participate in activities like olive picking and enjoy farm-to-table dining. This immersion in the rural lifestyle provides a unique perspective on Italy's agricultural heritage.

5. Language and Cultural Exchange: Deepen your cultural immersion by learning Italian. Participate in language classes or conversation groups, and consider homestays or volunteer opportunities. Living with an Italian family offers an authentic glimpse into daily life, traditions, and customs.

6. Nature and Outdoor Adventures: Italy's landscapes are a playground for outdoor enthusiasts. Hike the trails of the Amalfi Coast, kayak on Lake Como, or cycle through Tuscany's hills. These activities are not just about adventure; they're opportunities to connect with nature and local communities.

7. Historical Exploration in Rome: Wander through Rome's ancient ruins, like the Colosseum, and transport yourself to the era of gladiators. The city's rich history and monumental architecture are a testament to its timeless allure.

8. Artistic Journey in Florence: As the cradle of the Renaissance, Florence is a haven for art lovers. Marvel at masterpieces like Michelangelo's David in the Uffizi Gallery, immersing yourself in the city's artistic legacy.

9. Gastronomic Experience in Tuscany: Embrace Italy's culinary heart in Tuscany. Cooking classes here are not just about food; they're a celebration of local ingredients, traditional techniques, and the joy of Italian cooking.

10. Natural Beauty of the Amalfi Coast: The Amalfi Coast's stunning landscape is a haven for nature lovers. Explore this picturesque region by boat, uncover hidden coves, and experience the tranquility of its coastal beauty.

Each of these experiences offers a unique way to connect with Italy's culture, history, and natural beauty. By engaging in these activities, you'll gain a deeper understanding of Italy and create memories that last a lifetime. Pack your bags and prepare for an Italian adventure that goes beyond the ordinary, immersing you in the heart of this beautiful country.

Chapter 2: Northern Italy's Hidden Gems

2.1 Delights of Valle d'Aosta

In the embrace of the Italian Alps, where majestic peaks reach for the sky and verdant valleys whisper tales of yore, lies Valle d'Aosta, a hidden jewel in the crown of Italy's diverse regions. Nestled in the northwestern corner of the country, this region beckons with its blend of awe-inspiring natural beauty and a tapestry of rich cultural heritage, offering an escape into a world less traveled in Northern Italy.

Valle d'Aosta is not just a destination; it's an invitation to embark on a journey of discovery, where every winding path, secluded village, and ancient ruin tells a story. This is a land where the grandeur of nature meets the legacy of the past, where tranquility reigns supreme, and where the echoes of history resonate in the silent majesty of the mountains.

As we set out to explore Valle d'Aosta, we venture beyond the conventional tourist trails to uncover the secrets that this region guards so jealously. From quaint mountain hamlets to sacred sanctuaries nestled in breathtaking landscapes, from hidden trails leading to panoramic splendors to the artistic and historical wonders housed in its museums and galleries, Valle d'Aosta invites you to experience the authentic soul of Northern Italy.

In this journey through Valle d'Aosta, we are not merely sightseers; we are seekers of the extraordinary, delving into a realm where culture, history, and nature intertwine to create a tapestry of experiences that is as rich as it is rare. Join us as we traverse this land, savoring its culinary delights, reveling in its local customs, and unraveling the mysteries of its medieval villages and artisanal traditions. Valle d'Aosta is a region that promises not just sights to behold but memories to be cherished, an adventure that beckons to those who dare to wander off the beaten path.

Valle d'Aosta, nestled in the northwestern part of Italy, is truly an undiscovered gem. With its captivating natural beauty and rich cultural heritage, it promises an authentic and off-the-beaten-path adventure in Northern Italy.

As you embark on your journey through Valle d'Aosta, you'll find that this region holds hidden treasures beyond the well-known attractions. Here, we unveil some of the region's best-kept secrets, inviting you to explore its lesser-known wonders.

Mountain Villages: Beyond the bustling tourist spots lie charming mountain villages, each with its own unique charm. Wander through these traditional communities to experience the genuine local way of life.

In the culinary heart of Valle d'Aosta, indulge in the region's gastronomic treasures, where traditional flavors blend with the richness of the alpine environment. This region is celebrated for its distinctive cuisine, characterized by hearty dishes that resonate with the authenticity of mountain life.

Savor the renowned Fontina cheese, a staple of Valle d'Aosta's culinary tradition, known for its creamy texture and nutty flavor, an essential ingredient in local dishes like the warming Fonduta. The region's meats, such as lardo di Arnad and Jambon de Bosses, are delicacies that embody the art of Italian charcuterie.

Valle d'Aosta also takes pride in its unique wine production, with vineyards nestled in the picturesque landscapes. The local wines, like the robust reds of Torrette and the delicate whites of Blanc de Morgex et de La Salle, are a testament to the region's diverse terroir and winemaking heritage. A visit to one of the local vineyards offers not only a taste of these exquisite wines but also an insight into the winemaking process that has been honed over centuries.

Local dishes such as Carbonade, a savory stew made with locally sourced beef and wine, and Polenta Concia, a comforting dish enriched with cheese and butter, are culinary experiences that should not be missed. These dishes, often enjoyed in cozy mountain restaurants, reflect the deep connection between Valle d'Aosta's cuisine and its land.

As you journey through this enchanting region, let the flavors of Valle d'Aosta guide you to hidden culinary gems, offering a deeper understanding of this remarkable Italian territory. The region's cuisine, from its cheeses and meats to its unique wines, is an unspoken language that tells the story of Valle d'Aosta's culture and tradition.

Churches and Sanctuaries: Valle d'Aosta is home to a plethora of ancient churches and sanctuaries, often perched in breathtaking settings. The Church of San Martino in Gressoney-Saint-Jean and the Sanctuary of Cuney are particularly enchanting.

Scenic Trails: In addition to the renowned hiking routes, Valle d'Aosta boasts numerous hidden trails that lead to panoramic vistas. These less-traveled paths provide a tranquil way to immerse yourself in the region's natural beauty.

Museums and Art Galleries: Explore Valle d'Aosta's rich history, art, and culture through its museums and art galleries. The Regional Archaeological Museum in Aosta and the Museum S. Orso are just a couple of examples of the region's cultural treasures.

Local Cultural Events: Immerse yourself in the authentic local culture by attending traditional festivals, concerts, and theatrical performances. These events offer a glimpse into the vibrant traditions of Valle d'Aosta.

Medieval Villages: While Aosta is the most renowned, delve deeper into the region to discover equally captivating medieval villages like Bard and Fénis, where time seems to stand still.

Artisanal Products: Seek out small artisanal shops offering locally crafted goods such as textiles, ceramics, and gourmet products. Take home a piece of authentic Valle d'Aosta craftsmanship.

Less-Visited Valleys: Venture into the lesser-visited valleys like Valpelline and Valgrisenche, where you'll find pristine landscapes and a more serene atmosphere.

Sanctuary of San Besso: Tucked away in the Cogne Valley, this ancient sanctuary exudes a sense of spirituality amidst the surrounding mountains and forests.

Hidden Castles and Fortresses: Valle d'Aosta is adorned with not only famous castles but also lesser-known gems like the Sarriod de la Tour Castle, waiting to be explored.

As you traverse the region, remember to savor the culinary delights that Valle d'Aosta has to offer. Local specialties like fontina cheese and hearty dishes such as polenta and carbonade valdostana will tantalize your taste buds and offer a true taste of the region's culinary heritage.

Whether you're a history enthusiast, a nature lover, or a food connoisseur, Valle d'Aosta has something for everyone. Its stunning landscapes, rich history, and delicious cuisine make it a must-visit destination for those seeking an unforgettable and enriching experience in Northern Italy. So, pack your bags and embark on an adventure of discovery in this hidden gem of a region.

2.2 Unveiling the Charms of Piedmont

Tucked away in the northwest corner of Italy, where the majestic Alps meet the sky, Piedmont is a land of enchantment and allure. This region, a tapestry of verdant valleys, rolling vineyards, and historical cities, is Italy's well-kept secret, beckoning those in search of a journey less ordinary. Piedmont, with its unique blend of natural beauty, rich cultural heritage, and culinary excellence, invites travelers to embark on a captivating exploration of its many treasures.

In this chapter of our Italian voyage, we traverse the landscapes of Piedmont, from the elegant streets of its capital, Turin, to the hidden gems that dot its countryside. Here, in this corner of Italy, every hill, every village, and every vineyard tells a story steeped in history and draped in the beauty of nature.

Piedmont is not just a destination; it is an experience, a journey through a land where history and modernity dance in harmony, where nature's beauty is as profound as the flavors of its cuisine, and where the legacy of the past enriches the present. As we delve into the heart of Piedmont, we discover a world where the charm of the old world meets the vibrancy of the new, where every moment is a discovery, and every experience is a treasure.

From the sacred heights of the Sacra di San Michele, an ancient abbey inspiring tales and legends, to the tranquil shores of Lake Orta with its picturesque San Giulio Island, Piedmont reveals its hidden wonders. We wander through the well-preserved medieval streets of Ricetto di Candelo, and the historic city of Saluzzo, with its cobbled streets and ancient architecture. The renowned town of Alba, a gastronomic hub famous for its truffles and wines, offers a taste of Piedmont's rich culinary heritage.

The architectural grandeur of Piedmont unfolds before us in the majestic Castello di Fenis, with its well-preserved medieval structure and frescoed interiors. Nature enthusiasts are drawn to the breathtaking landscapes of the Parco Nazionale del Gran Paradiso, Italy's first national park, offering spectacular natural vistas and wildlife. The imposing Fortezza di Fenestrelle, known as the "Great Wall of Piedmont," and the serene Valle Maira, perfect for immersive nature walks, add to the region's diverse allure.

Piedmont's culinary and viticultural richness is unparalleled. Beyond the famous Barolo and Barbaresco wines, we indulge in the less-known yet exquisite Gattinara and Ghemme wines, robust reds from the northern reaches of Piedmont. The delicate Robiola di Roccaverano DOP cheese and the unique flavors of the Valli Occitane's cuisine, including "polenta concia" and "ravioles," showcase the region's diverse culinary influences.

In addition to the Robiola di Roccaverano, Piedmont's cheese heritage is a hidden treasure waiting to be explored. The region boasts an array of exquisite cheeses, each with its unique taste and story. The Toma Piemontese DOP, a semi-hard cheese with a delicate and slightly sweet flavor, is a testament to Piedmont's cheesemaking tradition. Another notable cheese is the Bra Duro, a hard cheese that can be savored in its young or mature form, each offering distinct textures and flavors.

The Castelmagno DOP, one of Italy's oldest cheeses, is a true gem of Piedmont's dairy production. This semi-hard, blue-veined cheese, with its strong and slightly spicy flavor, is perfect for enriching traditional dishes or enjoyed on its own. The region's Gorgonzola, a world-renowned blue cheese, known for its creamy texture and sharp taste, is another highlight of Piedmontese cheesemaking.

These cheeses not only reflect the diversity of Piedmont's culinary landscape but also tell a story of a land rich in dairy traditions, where cheesemaking is an art passed down through generations. Each cheese, whether enjoyed in a local trattoria or as part of a gourmet tasting, adds to the symphony of flavors that make Piedmont a haven for food enthusiasts

The area's viticulture is further celebrated through the elegant wines of Alto Piemonte, including appellations like Lessona and Bramaterra, which are gaining acclaim for their quality and uniqueness. The renowned Nocciola

Piemonte IGP hazelnuts, a cornerstone of local confectionery including the famous gianduiotto of Turin, highlight Piedmont's sweet delicacies.

Piedmontese cuisine shines in its variety of risottos, especially those flavored with truffles or Barolo wine. The communal dish of Bagna Càuda, a warm dip of garlic, anchovies, and olive oil, represents the convivial spirit of the region's food culture. Sweet treats made from hazelnut paste, like "Brutti ma Buoni" and "Baci di Dama," offer an authentic taste of Piedmont. The unique Erbaluce di Caluso wine, with its fresh and floral notes, and the traditional "Agnolotti del Plin", small pinched ravioli, round off the culinary journey.

In Piedmont, every experience is a journey through a land where history comes alive, nature enchants, and gastronomy delights. From the awe-inspiring architecture of Turin to the gastronomic wonders of Alba, Piedmont invites you to embark on a journey of discovery. Let Piedmont's captivating landscapes, rich history, and authentic flavors transport you to a realm of beauty and wonder. Join us in uncovering the hidden gems of Piedmont, a journey that promises to be as enriching as it is delightful.

2.3 Exploring the Enchanting Lakes of Lombardy

In the verdant embrace of northern Italy, where the Alps bow gently to meet the tranquil waters, lies the region of Lombardy – a tapestry of picturesque lakes and historic charm. Here, in this idyllic corner of Italy, the serene beauty of nature coalesces with the whispers of history to create a landscape that is as enchanting as it is diverse. As we embark on this journey through Lombardy, we invite you to discover the hidden gems and tranquil retreats nestled amidst its famous lakes and charming towns.

Lombardy is not just a region; it is a realm of serene escapes and captivating experiences. Each lake, from the renowned shores of Como to the expansive waters of Garda, and the majestic vistas of Maggiore, narrates a story of natural splendor and timeless allure. As we traverse this enchanting region, we uncover the secrets of its picturesque towns, immerse ourselves in its rich cultural tapestry, and revel in the tranquility of its natural landscapes.

This journey through Lombardy is an invitation to explore the lesser-known, yet equally mesmerizing, facets of this beautiful region. From the serene Lake Iseo to the historic streets of Bergamo Alta, the industrial heritage of Crespi d'Adda, and the prehistoric wonders of Val Camonica, each destination in Lombardy offers a unique glimpse into the heart and soul of northern Italy.

Join us as we set forth on this enchanting exploration of Lombardy's lakes – a journey that promises not just scenic beauty and relaxation but also a deep dive into the cultural and historical richness of this remarkable region. Let the tranquil waters, verdant hills, and charming villages of Lombardy captivate your heart and inspire your spirit.

A region in northern Italy that is home to some of the most enchanting lakes in the country. In this chapter, we will take you on a journey through the picturesque bodies of water that offer a tranquil and serene escape from the bustling cities. From the famous Lake Como to the expansive Lake Garda, each lake in Lombardy has its own unique charm and allure. Join us as we explore the stunning natural beauty, charming villages, and captivating experiences that await you in this idyllic region.

Lake Como, one of the most famous lakes in Lombardy, is renowned for its breathtaking scenery and luxurious villas. Nestled amidst the towering mountains, the crystal-clear waters of Lake Como reflect the surrounding landscape, creating a mesmerizing sight. The lake is dotted with charming towns and villages, such as Bellagio and Varenna, where visitors can explore cobblestone streets, indulge in delicious Italian cuisine, and soak in the laid-back atmosphere.

Another gem in Lombardy is Lake Garda, the largest lake in Italy. Known for its azure waters and mild climate, Lake Garda attracts visitors from all over the world. The lake is surrounded by picturesque towns like Sirmione, with its medieval castle and thermal baths, and Riva del Garda, famous for its charming harbor and vibrant waterfront. Outdoor enthusiasts can enjoy a variety of water sports, hiking trails, and cycling routes along the lake's shores.

Not to be missed is Lake Maggiore, a stunning lake located on the border between Italy and Switzerland. With its emerald green waters, magnificent islands, and luxurious villas, Lake Maggiore is a true paradise for nature lovers. The Borromean Islands, a group of small islands in the middle of the lake, are a must-visit attraction. Isola Bella, with its extravagant Baroque palace and stunning terraced gardens, is a highlight of any visit to Lake Maggiore.

Bergamo Alta, a historic jewel of the region, offers a unique experience with its well-preserved medieval architecture and stunning views. Wander through the ancient streets and squares, and immerse yourself in the rich history of this captivating city.

In Crespi d'Adda, visitors can step back in time and explore an exceptional example of an industrial village, reflecting the region's rich industrial heritage. The site, steeped in history, offers a unique perspective on the evolution of industry and community in Italy.

Lago d'Iseo, a serene and less-traveled destination, invites you to discover its beauty and the enchanting Monte Isola. The lake's tranquil waters and scenic surroundings make it an ideal spot for relaxation and nature exploration.

Val Camonica, renowned for its ancient rock carvings, offers a journey through time. The valley's prehistoric art is a testament to the region's long and fascinating history, providing a unique cultural experience.

The Certosa di Pavia, a masterpiece of Renaissance architecture, stands as a testament to the artistic and religious significance of the region. The complex's intricate design and peaceful atmosphere are a true delight for visitors.

Vigevano, with its impressive Piazza Ducale and rich history, offers a glimpse into the region's artistic and architectural splendor. The town's elegant layout and historical buildings make it a must-visit destination.

Exploring the lakes of Lombardy is like stepping into a postcard-perfect world. The region's natural beauty, combined with the charm of its lakeside towns and villages, creates an idyllic setting for a relaxing getaway. Whether you choose to cruise along the tranquil waters, hike through the surrounding hills, or simply unwind in a lakeside cafe, Lombardy's lakes will leave you enchanted and rejuvenated.

Sacred Mount of Varese, a blend of natural beauty and spiritual heritage, offers a peaceful retreat. The site's chapels and artwork, set amidst lush landscapes, provide a tranquil and reflective experience.

Gardone Riviera, situated on the shores of Lake Garda, is known for the Vittoriale degli Italiani, the extravagant residence of Gabriele D'Annunzio.

The town's beautiful gardens and historical significance make it a fascinating place to visit.

Soncino, a medieval village with its imposing fortress and picturesque setting, is a hidden gem. The town's ancient walls and historical charm offer a journey into the past, revealing the region's rich heritage.

Tirano and the Red Train of Bernina provide a spectacular journey through the Alps. The picturesque town of Tirano serves as the gateway to this unique rail experience, offering stunning views and unforgettable memories.

Brescia, often overlooked, is rich in history and art. The city's UNESCO World Heritage sites, including the San Salvatore-Santa Giulia monastery, showcase its cultural and historical depth.

In this exploration of Lombardy, beyond its enchanting natural landscapes and historical treasures, we invite you to discover the hidden culinary delights and exquisite wines that this region has to offer. Lombardy, known for its rich agricultural tradition, produces some of Italy's finest wines, such as the robust reds of Valtellina, known for their full-bodied and refined taste, and the elegant white wines of Franciacorta, celebrated for their delicacy and finesse.

The gastronomic journey through the region will lead you to unique local products, like the soft and aromatic Taleggio cheese, or the creamy and intense Gorgonzola. In towns and villages along the lakes and in the valleys, you can savor traditional dishes that tell the story and traditions of the local area, such as risotto alla milanese, famous for its rich flavor and distinctive golden color given by saffron, or polenta taragna, a warm and comforting dish typical of the Alpine valleys.

This journey through Lombardy is not just an opportunity to admire its scenic beauty and architectural treasures, but also to immerse yourself in its rich enogastronomic culture, discovering the authentic flavors that make this region truly special.

Whether you're seeking tranquility, adventure, or cultural experiences, the enchanting lakes of Lombardy are sure to captivate your heart and leave you with unforgettable memories. Plan your visit to Lombardy and immerse yourself in the natural beauty and charm of these mesmerizing lakes.

2.4 Discovering the Beauty of Liguria

In the embrace of the Italian Riviera, where the sea kisses the sky, lies the enchanting region of Liguria. A land of contrasts and hidden wonders, Liguria invites you on a journey through its picturesque towns, rugged cliffs, and azure waters. In this chapter, we explore the myriad treasures that this captivating coastal region has to offer, from the vibrant hues of Portofino to the serene beauty of Camogli, the rustic charm of Cinque Terre, and beyond.

Liguria is a tapestry woven with the threads of history, culture, and natural splendor. Each town, each village, each hidden cove tells a story, inviting travelers to immerse themselves in a world where the past and present dance in harmony. From the luxurious yachts of Portofino to the timeless trails of Cinque Terre, and the serene beaches of Camogli, Liguria is a symphony of experiences, a melody of sights, sounds, and flavors that beckon to be discovered.

Join us as we embark on this journey through Liguria, where every turn reveals a new wonder, every path leads to discovery, and every moment is a brushstroke on the canvas of the Italian Riviera. Let us uncover the hidden gems of this region, from the artistic streets of Bussana Vecchia to the medieval allure of Noli, the enchanting beauty of Valle Argentina, and the tranquil shores of Isola di Bergeggi. Liguria is not just a destination; it is a journey into the heart of Italy's coastal paradise, a journey that promises to captivate and enchant at every step.

One such gem is the enchanting town of Portofino. Nestled on a small peninsula, Portofino is famous for its colorful buildings, luxury yachts, and breathtaking views of the Mediterranean Sea. As you stroll along the waterfront promenade, you'll be greeted by a vibrant atmosphere filled with the scent of fresh seafood from the local restaurants. Indulge in delicious dishes made from the day's catch and savor the flavors of Ligurian cuisine. To delve into the town's past, visit the historic Castello Brown. This medieval fortress offers a glimpse into Portofino's rich history, with its well-preserved architecture and captivating exhibits. From the castle's vantage point, you can admire panoramic views of the town and the surrounding azure waters. It's a truly magical experience that transports you back in time.

Another hidden treasure in Liguria is the Cinque Terre, a collection of five picturesque fishing villages perched on the rugged cliffs of the Italian Riviera. Each village, including Monterosso al Mare, Vernazza, Corniglia, Manarola, and Riomaggiore, offers its own unique charm and character. Embark on a hike along the famous Sentiero Azzurro (Blue Trail) that connects the villages, and be rewarded with breathtaking views of the colorful houses, terraced vineyards, and the sparkling turquoise waters below. It's a journey that immerses you in the natural beauty of the region and allows you to appreciate the traditional way of life in these coastal communities.

For those seeking a quieter retreat, the town of Camogli is a hidden gem not to be missed. With its colorful buildings, pebbled beaches, and relaxed atmosphere, Camogli is the perfect place to unwind and soak in the beauty of the Ligurian coast. As you wander through the narrow streets, you'll come across charming gelaterias and trattorias offering delightful treats and local delicacies. Don't miss the opportunity to visit the 13th-century Basilica Santa Maria Assunta, an architectural wonder that showcases the region's rich religious heritage.

The hidden gem of Porto Venere, located at the southern end of the Cinque Terre, is another must-visit destination in Liguria. This picturesque seaside town is renowned for its historic buildings, including the striking Doria Castle and the beautiful Church of Saint Peter, perched on a rocky promontory overlooking the sea. Porto Venere's charming harbor, lined with brightly colored houses, offers a serene atmosphere for leisurely strolls and dining at waterside restaurants. The nearby Palmaria Island, accessible by a short boat ride, provides a peaceful escape with its unspoiled nature and scenic hiking trails.

In the Ligurian culinary odyssey, the region's food and wine hold a special place, telling a story of tradition and flavor. Liguria, with its rich maritime heritage, offers a treasure trove of gastronomic delights, from the fresh seafood of its coastal towns to the aromatic herbs that grow in its lush hinterlands.

In the bustling markets and quaint trattorias, experience the unique taste of traditional Ligurian dishes like trofie al pesto, a pasta dish made with fresh basil pesto that is a hallmark of the region. Another culinary gem is focaccia, a simple yet delicious flatbread that embodies the essence of Ligurian cuisine. In the coastal villages, don't miss trying the fresh anchovies, either marinated or fried, a staple of the local diet that captures the fresh flavors of the sea.

Liguria's wine tradition may be lesser-known but is equally enchanting. The region produces exquisite wines such as the crisp and refreshing Vermentino or the delicate Sciacchetrà, a sweet wine that is a perfect accompaniment to dessert or cheese. These wines are the result of centuries-old winemaking traditions, cultivated on the terraced hillsides that overlook the Mediterranean.

As you explore the charming town of Tellaro, take a moment to indulge in a glass of local wine, perhaps in a seaside cafe, and reflect on the rich tapestry of tastes and aromas that Liguria has to offer. This is a place where every meal is a celebration of the region's bountiful harvest, from land and sea.

Tellaro, a lesser-known yet equally enchanting destination, awaits with its tranquil charm and breathtaking sea views. This small fishing village is adorned with pastel-colored houses perched dramatically on the edge of the sea. The serene atmosphere here is perfect for those looking to escape the hustle and bustle of busier tourist spots.

Venture into the heart of Bussana Vecchia, a unique artist village born from the ruins of an old abandoned town. Here, art and history merge, creating an intriguing tapestry that tells stories of resilience and creativity. Wander through the narrow streets adorned with art galleries and studios, where each corner reveals a new discovery.

Noli, another coastal jewel, offers a blend of medieval history and picturesque beauty. This historic town is a hidden paradise for history enthusiasts, with its ancient walls and well-preserved castle offering a glimpse into Italy's storied past. The nearby beaches provide a peaceful setting for relaxation and reflection by the sea.

Experience the pristine natural beauty of Valle Argentina, where hiking trails lead through verdant landscapes and charming hilltop villages like Triora, known for its intriguing witchcraft history. The valley's unspoiled environment is a haven for nature lovers seeking solitude and tranquility.

In Apricale, one of Italy's most beautiful villages, you'll find yourself stepping into a scene from a fairy tale. The village's winding streets and traditional stone houses invite you to explore and uncover the secrets of its medieval charm.

Discover the underwater wonders and secluded beaches of Isola di Bergeggi, a haven for snorkelers and divers. This small island's natural reserve is a testament to the Ligurian coast's unspoiled beauty.

Finalborgo, nestled near Finale Ligure, is a well-preserved medieval gem that transports visitors back in time. Stroll through its ancient streets, where history resonates in every stone and archway.

Of course, the Ligurian coast is not just about its towns and villages. The region boasts stunning natural landscapes that are waiting to be explored. From the rugged cliffs of Cinque Terre to the expansive beaches of Camogli, nature lovers will find themselves in paradise.

Take a boat trip along the coast to discover hidden coves and secluded beaches, or venture into the lush Ligurian hinterland, where you'll find picturesque hiking trails and breathtaking vistas. Whether you're a history enthusiast, a food lover, or simply looking for a unique travel experience, Liguria has something to offer everyone. Discover the hidden beauty of this captivating region and create memories that will last a lifetime.

2.5 Unforgettable Experiences in Emilia-Romagna

In the heart of Italy, where the charm of history meets the richness of culture and the allure of gastronomy, lies Emilia-Romagna. This northern Italian region, a mosaic of vibrant cities, picturesque landscapes, and culinary wonders, beckons travelers to embark on a journey that is as diverse as it is enchanting. As we unveil the treasures of Emilia-Romagna, prepare to be immersed in a world where every corner tells a story, every dish brings a burst of flavor, and every moment captures the essence of Italian splendor.

Emilia-Romagna is not just a region; it is a gateway to experiences that blend the artistic mastery of the past with the lively pulse of the present. From the architectural marvels and historic streets of Bologna to the stunning mosaics of Ravenna, the region is a canvas of cultural and artistic expression. This journey through Emilia-Romagna is an invitation to explore beyond the surface, to delve into the heart of Italian tradition and beauty.

Join us as we traverse this captivating region, from the serene beauty of the

Apennine Mountains to the labyrinthine canals of Comacchio, the "Little Venice." Discover the charming medieval villages that dot the landscape, each with its unique character and story. Emilia-Romagna is a celebration of life, a feast for the senses, where the aroma of rich cuisine fills the air, and the beauty of nature soothes the soul.

Step into this enchanting world, where history, art, nature, and gastronomy intertwine to create a tapestry of experiences that are uniquely Italian. Welcome to Emilia-Romagna, where every discovery is a treasure, and every moment is a memory waiting to be cherished.

Welcome to Emilia-Romagna, a captivating region located in northern Italy that promises a journey filled with culinary delights, rich history, breathtaking art, and stunning natural landscapes. In this chapter, we will explore the diverse and unforgettable experiences that await travelers seeking to immerse themselves in the heart of Italian culture and beauty.

From the gastronomic wonders of Bologna to the mesmerizing mosaics of Ravenna, Emilia-Romagna offers a tapestry of experiences. Nature enthusiasts will be drawn to the picturesque landscapes of the Apennine Mountains and the Po River, and the region is peppered with charming medieval villages and unique architectural marvels.

The village of Dozza, with its colorful murals and medieval castle, transforms its streets into an open-air art gallery, offering a unique blend of history and creativity. Brisighella, with its cobbled streets, ancient mills, and the three hills crowned with a fortress, clock tower, and sanctuary, presents a picturesque medieval setting.

Comacchio, known as the "Little Venice," is a serene lagoon town characterized by canals and bridges. The Parco Regionale dei Sassi di Roccamalatina, with its spectacular rock formations, is a paradise for trekkers and nature lovers.

In the Valli di Comacchio, an extraordinary wetland area, visitors can enjoy birdwatching and exploring unspoiled nature. Castell'Arquato offers an imposing fortress and enchanting medieval streets. Monteveglio boasts stunning views of the surrounding park and a fascinating abbey.

Embark on a culinary journey through Emilia-Romagna, where the flavors of the region are as diverse and rich as its landscapes. This is the land where traditional Italian cuisine takes on new dimensions, offering an array of dishes and wines that are steeped in history and bursting with taste. The region is the birthplace of some of Italy's most celebrated culinary delights, including the iconic Parmigiano-Reggiano cheese, renowned worldwide for its distinct flavor and texture. Savor the rich and delicate taste of Prosciutto di Parma, a dry-cured ham that represents the pinnacle of Italian charcuterie.

Emilia-Romagna's cheese heritage extends far beyond the world-famous Parmigiano-Reggiano, offering a delightful array of flavors that are deeply rooted in the region's dairy tradition. One such hidden gem is the Squacquerone di Romagna DOP, a soft, creamy cheese with a mild and slightly tangy flavor, often enjoyed spread on piadina, a local flatbread. Another exquisite cheese is the Pecorino Romagnolo, a sheep's milk cheese that ranges from soft and delicate when young, to rich and robust as it ages, perfect for pairing with the region's wines.

As you meander through the rolling hills and quaint towns of Emilia-Romagna, be sure to seek out the Formaggio di Fossa di Sogliano DOP, a unique cheese aged in underground pits, acquiring a distinctive flavor profile that is both sharp and aromatic. This cheese is a testament to the inventive and time-honored techniques that define the region's cheesemaking heritage.

Each cheese of Emilia-Romagna tells its own story, offering a taste of the land and the local traditions that have shaped them. These artisanal cheeses are not only a delight for the palate but also embody the essence of the region's culinary artistry and history.

In the heart of Emilia-Romagna, the city of Modena beckons gourmands with its traditional balsamic vinegar, aged to perfection and known for its complex flavors and aroma. Discover the culinary treasure of Tortellini, a pasta delicacy filled with a blend of meat and cheese, born in the ancient streets of Bologna. In the town of Faenza, indulge in the unique cuisine influenced by its proximity to both the sea and the mountains, where every meal is a celebration of local ingredients and traditional cooking methods.

The region's wine culture is equally illustrious, with Emilia-Romagna producing some of the most exquisite and unique wines in Italy. Explore the vineyards of the Colli Piacentini, where the local grapes create delightful wines like Gutturnio and Ortrugo, reflecting the rich terroir of the area. The Sangiovese di Romagna, a robust and flavorful red wine, offers a taste of the region's passion for winemaking, while the sparkling Lambrusco, enjoyed worldwide, captures the lively spirit of Emilia-Romagna.

As you continue your exploration of Emilia-Romagna, let these culinary and oenological gems guide you through an unforgettable experience, where each sip and bite bring you closer to the heart of Italian gastronomic excellence.

Sant'Agata Feltria, the "town of fairies," features an enchanting medieval castle. Bagno di Romagna, renowned for its thermal baths, offers a tranquil wellness retreat. The UNESCO Biosphere Reserve of the Parco del Delta del Po showcases unique landscapes and rich biodiversity.

Rocca di Vignola and Nonantola, each with their significant history, stand as testaments to the region's rich past. Bertinoro offers panoramic views and exquisite wines. The Parco Nazionale dell'Appennino Tosco-Emiliano is a haven for nature lovers with its breathtaking landscapes.

The Castello di Torrechiara, with its Golden Room, is a highlight of the region's architectural heritage. Lastly, the Rocchetta Mattei, an architectural wonder with its eclectic style blending medieval, Moorish, and Gothic elements, offers a fascinating glimpse into the imagination of Count Cesare Mattei.

Each of these destinations in Emilia-Romagna, from tranquil lagoons to artistic villages and architectural wonders, adds depth to the region's allure. This captivating region invites you to immerse yourself in its culture, indulge in its flavors, and discover the beauty that lies within. Prepare for a journey that will tantalize your senses and create memories to last a lifetime.

2.6 Hidden Cultural Gems of Trentino-Alto Adige

In the shadow of the majestic Dolomites, where the air is crisp and the landscapes seem to leap out of a fairy tale, lies Trentino-Alto Adige, a region of northern Italy that beckons with its untold stories and hidden wonders. This journey through Trentino-Alto Adige is not just a passage through a region; it's an exploration of a cultural mosaic, a discovery of a land where history, nature, tradition, and gastronomic delights intertwine in the most enchanting ways.

Trentino-Alto Adige, with its blend of Italian and Austrian influences, offers a unique cultural tapestry that is as diverse as its landscapes. From the imposing Castel Thun and Castel Beseno, guardians of history and tradition, to medieval villages such as Rango and Canale di Tenno, where time seems to stand still amidst their cobbled streets and festive markets, this region invites you to uncover its lesser-known yet equally mesmerizing facets.

Our journey takes us through verdant valleys and towering peaks, revealing new wonders at every turn. The Parco Naturale Paneveggio - Pale di San Martino, with its spectacular rock formations and lush forests, offers trails for wildlife viewing, while the Museo Archeologico delle Palafitte di Fiavé provides a fascinating glimpse into the region's prehistoric life. The majestic Castel Beseno, near Trento, invites us to walk through corridors echoing with medieval tales.

We pause at the serene Lake Tovel in the Adamello Brenta Nature Park, known for its unique "red tide" phenomenon, and the idyllic Val di Funes, a picturesque valley offering breathtaking views of the Dolomites and traditional alpine churches. Lake Carezza, with its crystal-clear waters and vivid colors, adds a mystical element to the region's beauty.

The charming towns and villages, including Bressanone (Brixen), one of Tyrol's oldest cities, and Merano, a spa town blending Austrian and Italian influences, showcase the region's rich history and cultural diversity. The Val di Non, celebrated for its apple orchards, enchants visitors with its agritourism experiences, and the Giardini di Castel Trauttmansdorff in Merano offers a blend of various botanical zones against a backdrop of stunning mountains.

In Rovereto, cultural heritage shines at the Museum of Modern and Contemporary Art (MART) and the Bell of the Fallen, a significant peace monument. San Martino di Castrozza, beyond its alpine charm, is a haven for hiking and winter sports enthusiasts, set against stunning Dolomite panoramas.

The culinary journey becomes an integral part of the exploration in Trentino-Alto Adige. Local cheese varieties like Trentingrana and Casolét, traditional bakeries, and local markets offer an array of artisanal delights, reflecting centuries of culinary tradition. The region's vineyards, producing exquisite wines like Gewürztraminer and Pinot Grigio, offer unique tasting experiences.

These hidden gems of Trentino-Alto Adige offer a rich and varied experience, inviting visitors to discover not only the beauty and cultural wealth of this fascinating Italian region but also its extraordinary culinary landscape. Beyond its natural allure, Trentino-Alto Adige is a mosaic of history, art, tradition, and gastronomy, a cultural and culinary journey for those seeking to venture off the beaten path. Whether delving into ancient castles, absorbing stories in museums and art galleries, indulging in local culinary traditions, or exploring the vineyards, Trentino-Alto Adige promises an adventure that will captivate and enchant.

2.7 Discover the Hidden Wonders and Timeless Beauty of Veneto

In the northeastern embrace of Italy, where the gentle plains gracefully meet the Adriatic Sea's shimmering waters, lies a land of enchantment and allure – Veneto. This region, a splendid mosaic of historical cities, serene landscapes, and vine-clad hills, is Italy's hidden jewel, a treasure trove of experiences waiting for the discerning traveler. Veneto, with its mesmerizing blend of natural splendor, rich cultural heritage, and culinary excellence, invites you to embark on an exploration that transcends the ordinary.

As we embark on this captivating journey through Veneto, we venture beyond the renowned splendor of Venice and Verona, delving into the heart of a region brimming with stories, flavors, and sights that defy the expectations of even the most seasoned traveler. Here, each town, each monument, and each natural wonder tells a tale of time's passage, offering a glimpse into a world where history, art, and nature intertwine in an intricate dance.

Our adventure begins with the enchanting towns sprinkled across Veneto's landscape. Asolo, "The City of a Hundred Horizons," welcomes us with its picturesque medieval charm, while Marostica, with its living chess tradition, brings history to life in its vibrant main square. We wander through the well-preserved streets of Arquà Petrarca, once a haven for the poet Francesco Petrarca, and feel the artistic pulse of Bassano del Grappa, renowned for its Palladian bridge and traditional grappa production. Chioggia, often referred to as "Little Venice," captures our hearts with its authentic canals and lively fishing town atmosphere.

The journey through Veneto's towns is not complete without a visit to the peaceful Isola di San Francesco del Deserto, nestled in the Venetian lagoon, and Cittadella, one of Europe's few medieval towns with fully intact defensive walls. We also find ourselves captivated by the tranquility of the Parco Naturale Regionale dei Colli Euganei, with its volcanic hills and scenic trails, and the rolling landscapes of Valdobbiadene and Conegliano, the heartlands of Prosecco production.

As we delve deeper into Veneto, its architectural wonders and historical monuments reveal themselves. Villa Emo in Fanzolo and Villa Barbaro in Maser, both designed by the illustrious Andrea Palladio, enchant us with their Renaissance beauty and exquisite frescoed interiors. The Tempio Canoviano in Possagno, a neoclassical marvel by Antonio Canova, offers a window into the sculptor's grand legacy. The Cathedral of Santa Maria Annunciata in Vicenza, a harmonious blend of Gothic and Renaissance styles, and the Castello del Catajo in Battaglia Terme, a fusion of Venetian villa charm and medieval fortress strength, leave us in awe of Veneto's diverse architectural heritage. The Oratorio di San Giorgio in Padua and the Teatro Olimpico in Vicenza, each a testament to the artistic richness of the region, beckon with their historical significance.

Our architectural tour wouldn't be complete without marveling at the Scaliger Tombs in Verona and La Rotonda in Rovigo, each echoing tales from the past in their unique way.

In Veneto, the journey of discovery extends to the realm of taste. The region's culinary scene, as diverse as its landscapes, presents an array of traditional dishes that capture the essence of Veneto's rich agricultural heritage. From the succulent seafood of the Adriatic coast to the comforting flavors of polenta and risotto of the inland areas, each meal is a celebration of local culinary artistry. The region is also a haven for cheese connoisseurs, with Asiago and Monte Veronese adding distinct notes to the Venetian gastronomic symphony.

A pivotal aspect of Veneto's charm is its esteemed winemaking tradition. Here, the rolling hills of Valdobbiadene and Conegliano not only offer stunning views but also produce the world-renowned Prosecco, a symbol of

Italian celebration and elegance. The region's wines, including Valpolicella, Soave, and Amarone, are a harmonious blend of tradition and innovation, reflecting the passion and expertise of its vintners. A visit to Veneto's wineries and cantinas is more than a tasting experience; it's a journey into the heart of the region's vinicultural legacy.

In Veneto, every step is a discovery, every flavor a revelation, and every sight a memory in the making. This journey through Veneto invites you to explore a region where history is alive, nature's beauty is overwhelming, and culinary delights are abundant. Join us on this enchanting exploration of Veneto, a hidden gem in Italy's crown, waiting to share its stories, flavors, and beauty with the world.

2.8 Off-the-Beaten-Path in Friuli-Venezia Giulia

In the northeastern corner of Italy, where the allure of the Adriatic Sea meets the mystique of the Alps, lies Friuli-Venezia Giulia, a region rich in diversity and hidden wonders. This chapter of our Italian adventure takes us through a landscape where history is etched into ancient Roman ruins, nature unfolds in lush parks and towering mountains, and culture is savored in every bite of its renowned cuisine.

Friuli-Venezia Giulia is not just a region; it's a tapestry of experiences, a blend of the majestic and the intimate, where each town, each natural reserve, and each culinary tradition tells a story of a land shaped by a myriad of influences. From the intricate mosaics of Aquileia to the star-shaped fortress of Palmanova, and from the awe-inspiring Grotte Giganti to the serene beauty of the Dolomiti Friulane, this journey invites you to uncover the lesser-known yet equally captivating facets of this enchanting region.

Join us as we explore Friuli-Venezia Giulia, where every corner reveals a new surprise, every path leads to discovery, and every flavor brings a taste of the region's rich heritage. Let us delve into the heart of this diverse region, where history, nature, and gastronomy come together to create a mosaic of unforgettable experiences. Welcome to Friuli-Venezia Giulia, a hidden gem of Italy waiting to share its secrets with those who seek to uncover them.

When exploring the picturesque region of Friuli-Venezia Giulia in Northern Italy, you're in for a treat beyond the well-known destinations like Trieste and

Udine. There exists a hidden world of charming gems waiting to be discovered, offering a delightful journey filled with history, culture, nature, and gastronomy.

Aquileia is a testament to time, where the remnants of an ancient Roman city and stunning paleo-Christian mosaics create a vivid picture of the past. Recognized by UNESCO, it invites you to step back into history.

Palmanova stands out with its unique star-shaped fortress design, a Renaissance marvel of military architecture that captivates the imagination with its meticulous planning and historical significance.

The Grotte Giganti of Sgonico offers an adventure beneath the earth. These vast caves reveal awe-inspiring geological formations, a natural wonder that showcases the region's unique subterranean beauty.

The Dolomiti Friulane Natural Park is a haven for nature enthusiasts. Its untouched landscapes and rugged beauty provide a peaceful escape and a chance to explore the lesser-known Dolomites.

Valbruna and Lake Predil present a blend of natural beauty and historical intrigue. They offer a perfect setting for outdoor activities, with a backdrop rich in stories from the Great War.

The Karst Plateau near Trieste mesmerizes with its unique topography. Explore its trails and discover hidden caves, including the remarkable Grotta Gigante, in a landscape that combines natural wonder with scientific fascination.

Spilimbergo is known for its world-class mosaic school and vibrant town center. It's a place where art comes alive, both in the streets and in the intricate mosaics that adorn them.

Miramare Castle in Trieste is not just a historical building but a narrative of love and dreams. The castle, surrounded by a luxuriant botanical park, overlooks the Gulf of Trieste, offering breathtaking views and a glimpse into royal life.

The Julian Prealps Nature Park invites you to explore its diverse landscapes, from serene meadows to rugged mountain terrain, offering a sanctuary for diverse flora and fauna.

The Isonzo River Mouth Nature Reserve is a paradise for bird watchers and nature lovers. The lush wetlands are home to a rich array of bird species, making it an ideal spot for peaceful exploration and wildlife observation.

The Celestial Pathway is more than a trail; it's a spiritual journey linking sacred sites in the region and extending into Slovenia, offering a unique blend of nature and contemplation.

The Rilke Trail near Duino enchants with its coastal views and poetic inspiration. It's a path that not only offers scenic beauty but also a connection to the literary world.

San Daniele del Friuli is renowned for its exquisite prosciutto, but it's also a charming town with panoramic views and a rich history waiting to be explored.

Venzone, celebrated for its medieval walls and the Cathedral of Santa Maria Assunta, becomes a festival of colors and flavors during the annual Pumpkin Festival. This event encapsulates the village's vibrant culture and community spirit.

Val Rosandra Nature Reserve, a stone's throw from Trieste, is a natural oasis with scenic hiking trails, limestone cliffs, and tranquil spots perfect for nature lovers seeking a serene getaway.

Collio, a paradise for wine enthusiasts, invites you to explore its vineyards. Known for exceptional white wines, it's a journey through the art of winemaking, where each sip tells a story of tradition and terroir.

The Wine and Flavors Route of Friuli Venezia Giulia opens a world of culinary delights. Traverse vineyards and farms, tasting the region's specialties and immersing yourself in a sensory journey through its gastronomic landscape.

In addition to these experiences, the region's culinary journey is deepened by exploring its lesser-known yet exquisite gastronomic offerings. Discover the hidden world of Friuli's cured meats beyond the famous San Daniele prosciutto, with specialties like Pitina, a smoked meatball made from game meat. Venture into the vineyards of the Colli Orientali del Friuli, where the local winemakers craft exceptional wines that reflect the unique terroir of the area. In this journey, every sip and every bite bring you closer to the heart and soul of Friuli-Venezia Giulia's rich gastronomic culture.

These hidden gems of Friuli-Venezia Giulia promise a journey filled with cherished memories and a profound appreciation for the rich tapestry that makes this Italian region remarkable. Each destination, whether it be a historical town, a natural reserve, or a culinary hotspot, contributes to the unforgettable mosaic of experiences that define Friuli-Venezia Giulia.

Chapter 3: Central Italy's Hidden Gems

3.1 Uncovering the Secrets of Tuscany

In the heart of Italy, where rolling hills meet historic towns and art intersects with nature, lies Tuscany. This celebrated region, renowned for its cultural landmarks and natural beauty, offers far more than the iconic images of cypress-lined roads and Renaissance art. Beyond the well-trodden paths of Florence, Siena, and Pisa, Tuscany harbors a myriad of hidden gems, each with its own unique story and charm. As we embark on this journey through Tuscany, let us uncover these lesser-known yet equally enchanting towns and landscapes, inviting you to explore the depth and diversity of this magnificent region.

Tuscany is not just a destination; it is a mosaic of experiences, a journey through a landscape where every hilltop, every valley, and every town is steeped in history and beauty. From the tranquility of Fiesole's hills to the medieval streets of San Miniato, the Renaissance charm of Lucca, and the timeless allure of the Chianti region, Tuscany is a treasure trove waiting to be explored.

Join us as we venture into the heart of Tuscany, where hidden villages like Poppi and Arezzo offer a glimpse into the region's rich past, and towns like Montepulciano and Montalcino beckon with their world-renowned wines. Discover the idyllic beauty of Pienza, the tranquility of San Quirico d'Orcia, the medieval towers of San Gimignano, and the Etruscan legacy of Chiusi. Let us take you to Vinci, where the genius of Leonardo da Vinci comes alive, and to the soothing waters of Bagno Vignoni.

This journey through Tuscany is an invitation to experience the region beyond its postcard-perfect landscapes, to delve into the heart of its culture, history, and natural beauty. Welcome to a world where every corner holds a delightful surprise, every town tells a story, and every experience enriches the soul. Welcome to the hidden Tuscany, a land of undiscovered wonders.

Tuscany, nestled in the heart of central Italy, is a region that has earned worldwide acclaim for its rich history, breathtaking landscapes, and unparalleled art and architecture. It stands as a testament to the splendor of Italy. While the cities of Florence, Siena, and Pisa often steal the spotlight, there exists a treasure trove of hidden gems within this captivating region, waiting to be discovered by intrepid travelers.

In the town of Florence, we find Fiesole, a peaceful hilltop retreat offering stunning panoramic views of the Tuscan capital. Immerse yourself in its rich history, visit the ancient Roman theater, and explore the picturesque streets that wind through the town.

Another hidden gem in Tuscany is San Miniato, boasting breathtaking views and a fascinating history. Marvel at the medieval architecture that adorns the town and indulge in its culinary delights, which include delectable truffles.

Venture to Lucca, a city that exudes Renaissance charm. Walk along its intact city walls and lose yourself in the picturesque cobblestone streets. Take your time to enjoy leisurely strolls, explore historical landmarks, and soak in the city's unique atmosphere.

Travel back in time to the Middle Ages as you explore the charming village of Poppi. Admire the imposing Poppi Castle, a magnificent example of medieval architecture. Wander through its historic center, where every corner tells a story, and experience the rich history and culture that permeate this enchanting place.

Discover Arezzo, a town with a rich artistic heritage. Marvel at its stunning frescoes, explore the grandeur of the Piazza Grande, and delve into the town's vibrant cultural scene. Don't miss the chance to visit the famous Basilica of San Francesco with its remarkable cycle of frescoes by Piero della Francesca.

Explore Gaiole in Chianti, surrounded by vineyards and olive groves. This town serves as the perfect base for exploring the beautiful Chianti countryside. Immerse yourself in the scenic landscapes, visit local wineries, and experience the authentic Tuscan lifestyle.

Visit Radda in Chianti, nestled in the heart of the famous Chianti wine region. Not only does it offer a picturesque setting, but also the opportunity to savor world-class wines. Explore the charming old town, stroll through vineyards, and indulge in the delights of Tuscan cuisine.

Discover Castellina in Chianti, surrounded by rolling hills and vineyards. Explore its charming old town, adorned with medieval walls and historical landmarks. Indulge in delicious local cuisine, sample renowned wines, and soak in the idyllic Tuscan countryside.

Next on our Tuscan exploration is Siena, a city that truly embodies the medieval spirit. Lose yourself in its labyrinthine streets, marvel at the magnificent Piazza del Campo, and delve into the rich history and cultural heritage that permeate every corner.

Continuing our journey, we find Montepulciano, an enchanting hilltop town renowned for its exquisite wines. Take in the breathtaking views of the surrounding countryside as you indulge in wine tastings and explore the town's charming streets.

For wine enthusiasts, Montalcino is a mandatory stop on your Tuscan journey. Nestled amid the rolling hills, this picturesque town is renowned for producing Italy's illustrious Brunello di Montalcino wine. Embark on an exploration of vineyards that stretch as far as the eye can see and gain insight into the winemaking process from passionate local vintners.

Step into the picturesque town of Pienza and be transported to the Renaissance era. Known as the "Ideal City," Pienza is renowned for its well-preserved architecture and stunning views of the rolling Val d'Orcia.

Amidst the rolling hills and medieval towns, Tuscany's culinary delights stand as a testament to its rich gastronomic heritage. This land, famous for its robust wines and flavorful cuisine, offers a journey of taste that complements its scenic beauty. Savor the exquisite Chianti and Brunello di Montalcino, wines celebrated globally for their depth and complexity, born from the fertile vineyards that blanket the Tuscan countryside.

The region's cheese-making tradition is equally illustrious, with hidden gems like Pecorino Toscano DOP, a sheep's milk cheese with a nutty flavor and firm texture, and the creamy and delicate Marzolino. These cheeses are a product of age-old techniques, perfected in the pastoral landscapes of Tuscany.

Tuscan cuisine, characterized by its simplicity and reliance on fresh, high-quality ingredients, invites you to indulge in traditional dishes like ribollita, a hearty vegetable and bread soup, and pappa al pomodoro, a flavorful tomato and bread dish. In the heart of Tuscany, discover the unique flavors of wild boar dishes, a local specialty, and the exquisite white truffles of San Miniato, a culinary treasure hidden within the region's verdant forests.

As you journey through the towns of San Quirico d'Orcia and beyond, each meal becomes an exploration of Tuscany's rich culinary landscape, a delightful experience that is as soul-satisfying as its art and natural beauty.

Immerse yourself in the tranquility of San Quirico d'Orcia, a charming village dotted with medieval walls and ancient churches. Take a leisurely stroll along its cobblestone streets and discover hidden corners that exude a timeless atmosphere.

One such hidden gem is the town of San Gimignano. Its medieval towers, which dominate the skyline, transport you to a bygone era. The town's thirteen towering medieval structures, once fortified defenses, now stand as a picturesque reminder of its storied history.

Another hidden treasure in Tuscany is the town of Cortona, made famous by the book and movie 'Under the Tuscan Sun.' Perched on a hilltop, this enchanting town offers sweeping vistas of the surrounding countryside.

Further into the heart of Tuscany, we reach Chiusi, an ancient Etruscan town that transports you back in time. Discover its archaeological treasures, including underground tunnels, and learn about the fascinating civilization that once thrived here.

Uncover the genius of Leonardo da Vinci in his birthplace, Vinci. Visit the Leonardo Museum and delve into the life and works of one of history's greatest minds. Take a walk through the enchanting Tuscan countryside that inspired the artist.

Indulge in relaxation and wellness in the thermal village of Bagno Vignoni. Immerse yourself in its thermal waters, known for their therapeutic properties since ancient times.

Step into the past as you enter Monteriggioni, a perfectly preserved medieval walled town. Marvel at its imposing walls and towers, which offer breathtaking panoramic views of the surrounding countryside.

Explore the coastal village of Castiglion della Pescaia, a popular seaside resort offering pristine beaches, crystal-clear waters, and a charming old town. Relax by the sea, indulge in delicious seafood, and soak up the coastal ambiance.

Discover Pitigliano, a town perched atop a tufa ridge. Its narrow alleys, ancient caves, and stunning views of the surrounding countryside will enchant and captivate you. Immerse yourself in the town's history and marvel at its unique architecture.

Journey to Massa Marittima, nestled in the Maremma region. Its medieval charm, impressive cathedral, and panoramic vistas make it a must-visit destination. Explore the town's historical sites, immerse yourself in its rich heritage, and soak in the breathtaking views.

Relax in Saturnia, renowned for its healing thermal baths. This oasis of relaxation and rejuvenation offers the perfect escape from the hustle and bustle of everyday life. Immerse yourself in the warm, mineral-rich waters and let your worries melt away.

Visit Anghiari, known for its picturesque streets and historic buildings. Experience a delightful mix of art, history, and natural beauty as you stroll through its charming streets and admire its architectural treasures.

Wander through Sarteano, a charming hilltop village. Visit its ancient castle, immerse yourself in its rich history, and discover the town's unique cultural heritage.

Finally, in the Garfagnana Valley, explore Castelnuovo di Garfagnana, a town that offers both medieval charm and breathtaking mountain views. Explore its medieval fortress, wander through its charming streets, and immerse yourself in the natural beauty that surrounds the area.

As you traverse through these enchanting Tuscan towns, you'll be captivated by their historical significance, artistic treasures, and natural wonders. Each destination offers a unique experience, allowing you to truly immerse yourself in the beauty and cultural heritage of Tuscany.

3.2 Discover the Hidden Gems of Umbria, the 'Green Heart of Italy

In the green heart of Italy, where the rolling hills whisper stories of the past and the landscapes paint a picture of serene beauty, lies Umbria. This enchanting region, nestled away from the bustling tourist tracks, invites you on a journey filled with discovery, wonder, and tranquility. Umbria, often overshadowed by its more famous neighbors, holds within its borders an array of hidden treasures that beckon to be explored by those who seek the authentic essence of Italy.

Umbria is not just a region; it's a mosaic of experiences, a haven where history, culture, nature, and gastronomy intertwine to create an unforgettable tapestry of travel memories. From the ancient streets of Perugia to the mystical allure of Assisi, the architectural marvels of Orvieto, and the untouched beauty of the Apennine Mountains, Umbria offers a diverse palette of experiences to all who wander its paths.

Join us as we embark on this journey through Umbria, where every town, every landscape, and every dish tells a story of a land rich in history and brimming with beauty. Let us uncover the secrets of this hidden gem, where the warmth of its people, the charm of its towns, and the splendor of its natural settings create a symphony of experiences that capture the true spirit of Italy. Welcome to Umbria, a journey into the heart of Italy's hidden beauty.

Umbria, nestled in the heart of Italy, is a hidden gem waiting to be discovered by travelers seeking an authentic and immersive experience. This region captivates visitors with its stunning landscapes, rich history, and warm hospitality, making it a true treasure of Italy. Umbria's natural beauty is nothing short of spectacular. Its picturesque landscapes feature rolling hills, serene valleys, and shimmering lakes that seem like they've been plucked from a postcard. This diverse terrain provides a playground for outdoor enthusiasts, offering opportunities for hiking, biking, and even hot air balloon rides to soak in the panoramic vistas that stretch as far as the eye can see. Steeped in history, Umbria is a treasure trove of ancient ruins, medieval castles, and Renaissance architecture. The hilltop towns scattered across the region offer a captivating glimpse into the past.

When you visit Perugia, Assisi, or Orvieto, you'll find yourself meandering through narrow cobblestone streets, quaint piazzas, and centuries-old churches that transport you to another era. Umbria's warm hospitality is a defining feature of the region. The locals are known for their genuine friendliness and welcoming nature, and visitors are often embraced like old friends. Immerse yourself in the vibrant local culture by partaking in traditional festivals, exploring lively markets, or indulging in authentic farm-to-table dining experiences. For wine connoisseurs, Umbria is a paradise. The region's vineyards produce some of Italy's most exquisite wines, including Sagrantino, Grechetto, and Orvieto Classico. Wine tastings and vineyard tours offer a chance to learn about the winemaking process while indulging in the rich flavors and aromas of Umbria. To delve deeper into the enchantment of Umbria, let's explore a few of its hidden treasures: Ancient Hilltop Towns: Umbria's hilltop towns are a highlight of the region.

Assisi, the birthplace of St. Francis, boasts the magnificent Basilica di San Francesco, a UNESCO World Heritage site.

Gubbio enchants with its well-preserved medieval architecture, including the iconic Palazzo dei Consoli, providing panoramic views of the surrounding landscape. Gastronomic Delights: Umbria is a haven for food lovers. Savor the renowned black truffles, foraged in the lush forests surrounding the towns. Dive into the rich and creamy flavors of Umbrian olive oil, celebrated for its exceptional quality. Don't miss the opportunity to try porchetta, a succulent slow-roasted pork dish seasoned with fragrant herbs and spices. Pair your meal with a glass of Sagrantino, the region's famous red wine, and embark on a journey of culinary delight.

Explore Lush Vineyards: Umbria's vineyards offer a sensory adventure. Stroll through the vine-covered hills, taking in the beauty of the landscape. Visit family-run wineries, where passionate winemakers will guide you through tastings, sharing their love for winemaking. Sample the robust and full-bodied Sagrantino, the jewel of Umbria's wine culture. Immerse Yourself in History:

Umbria's rich history comes to life through ancient ruins and architectural marvels.

Explore the Roman remnants in Spoleto, including the remarkable Roman theater and the iconic Ponte delle Torri, a towering bridge offering breathtaking views.

In Perugia, the regional capital, delve into its cultural heritage by visiting the Palazzo dei Priori, an exquisite Gothic palace that houses the National Gallery of Umbria, home to masterpieces by renowned Italian artists.

Discover Todi: Todi, a charming hill town in Umbria, welcomes visitors with its medieval architecture and breathtaking views of the surrounding countryside. Explore the picturesque streets, visit the stunning Cathedral of Todi, and experience the town's vibrant cultural scene.

Experience Norcia: Nestled in the Sibillini Mountains, Norcia is renowned for its gastronomic traditions, including the famous Norcia black truffle. Explore the town's historic center, visit the Basilica of St. Benedict, and indulge in the local delicacies.

In the heart of Umbria, the region's cuisine is a celebration of its rich agricultural heritage, offering an array of gastronomic delights that encapsulate the essence of Italian cooking. Umbria is particularly renowned for its exquisite wines, including the robust and tannic Sagrantino di Montefalco and the versatile and fragrant Orvieto Classico. These wines, born from the fertile hills and vineyards of the region, reflect the unique terroir and centuries-old winemaking traditions of Umbria.

Umbrian cheese-making is an art in itself, with local varieties such as Pecorino Umbro, a sheep's milk cheese that ranges from soft and delicate to aged and flavorful, providing a true taste of the region's dairy craftsmanship. The fresh and creamy Raviggiolo, often used in traditional dishes, is another testament to the region's cheese-making excellence.

Indulge in the culinary specialties that define Umbrian cuisine, from the savory and succulent porchetta, a seasoned and slow-roasted pork dish, to the hearty and flavorsome umbricelli pasta, often served with a truffle or meat sauce. Let the rich and earthy flavors of Umbria's black truffles tantalize your taste buds, a prized ingredient that elevates any dish with its distinctive aroma and taste.

As you explore the verdant landscapes and medieval towns of Umbria, take the opportunity to dine in local trattorias and osterias where traditional recipes are prepared with passion and flair, offering an authentic and unforgettable dining experience. Each meal in Umbria is not just a feast for the palate but a journey into the heart of its culinary traditions and local culture.

Discover the Enchantment of Castelluccio di Norcia: Nestled in the heart of Umbria, the mesmerizing village of Castelluccio di Norcia is a hidden treasure waiting to unveil its beauty to the discerning traveler. Perched at an altitude of over 1,450 meters, Castelluccio boasts some of the most spectacular panoramic views in Italy, with its lush, undulating plains set against the majestic backdrop of the Sibillini Mountains. This quaint village, one of the highest in the Apennines, is renowned for the breathtaking phenomenon of "La Fiorita," an annual event where its fields burst into a vibrant display of colors with the blooming of lentils, poppies, daisies, and other wildflowers. The charm of Castelluccio lies not only in its natural beauty but also in its rich history and cultural heritage. Wander through the narrow streets of this medieval village to discover a timeless world, where age-old traditions are still a part of everyday life. The ruins of the ancient fortifications tell a tale of a past that has withstood the test of time.

Unwind at Lago Trasimeno: Lago Trasimeno, Italy's fourth-largest lake, offers a tranquil retreat surrounded by lush nature. Relax on its shores, take a boat tour to explore the islands, and savor fresh fish dishes in the charming lakeside towns.

Visit Spello: Spello, a picturesque hill town adorned with vibrant flowers, is a delight to wander through. Discover its well-preserved Roman walls, admire the beautiful frescoes in the Church of Santa Maria Maggiore, and soak in the enchanting atmosphere.

Explore Bevagna: Bevagna, a medieval town in the heart of Umbria, transports visitors back in time with its well-preserved architecture and charming squares. Explore the Roman remains, visit the stunning Piazza Silvestri, and immerse yourself in the town's rich history.

Discover Montefalco: Montefalco, known as the "Balcony of Umbria," offers breathtaking views of the surrounding vineyards and valleys. Visit the impressive Montefalco Cathedral, explore the town's narrow streets, and indulge in the region's renowned Sagrantino wine.

Witness Cascata delle Marmore: Cascata delle Marmore, one of Italy's most stunning waterfalls, is a must-visit natural wonder. Admire the cascading waters, take a scenic hike in the surrounding nature reserve, and marvel at the breathtaking beauty of the falls.

Explore Orvieto Underground: Beneath the charming town of Orvieto lies a labyrinth of underground tunnels and caves. Take a guided tour to discover the ancient Etruscan and medieval structures, including wells, cellars, and even a subterranean church.

Umbria offers a wealth of experiences, from natural beauty and historical wonders to delectable cuisine and warm hospitality. It's a destination that promises to leave an indelible mark on your heart, inviting you to explore its hidden gems and create lasting memories.

3.3 Exploring the Authenticity of Marche

In the heart of Italy, nestled between the rolling hills of the Apennines and the gentle waves of the Adriatic Sea, lies the region of Marche. A hidden treasure of Italy, Marche offers a journey through a landscape of unspoiled beauty, rich history, and authentic Italian culture. This region, often overlooked by the well-trodden tourist paths, invites you to discover a world where the charm of medieval towns, the splendor of natural wonders, and the warmth of Italian hospitality come together in perfect harmony.

Marche is not just a destination; it's an experience, a chance to immerse yourself in the authentic essence of Italy. From the awe-inspiring Frasassi Caves to the storied walls of Gradara, the sacred Basilica in Loreto, and the poetic streets of Recanati, Marche weaves a tapestry of experiences that beckon the traveler seeking something beyond the ordinary.

Join us on this journey through Marche, where every hill, every coastline, and every town tells a story of a land steeped in history and brimming with beauty. Let us discover the hidden gems of Marche, where nature's artistry, cultural riches, and culinary delights await at every turn. Welcome to Marche, a journey into the heart of Italy's lesser-known yet equally enchanting region.

The region of Marche, located in central Italy, is a hidden gem that offers a truly authentic Italian experience. Nestled between the Apennine Mountains and the Adriatic Sea, Marche is known for its picturesque landscapes, charming medieval towns, and rich cultural heritage. Discover a sense of authenticity often missed in more popular tourist destinations as you explore this lesser-known region.

Marche's diverse and untouched natural beauty ranges from rolling hills covered in vineyards to rugged mountains and pristine beaches. Nature enthusiasts will find ample opportunities for outdoor activities such as hiking, cycling, and immersing in the tranquil beauty of unspoiled beaches.

Uncover the mysteries of the Frasassi Caves, an awe-inspiring subterranean wonder, revealing nature's artistry in the form of intricate stalactites and stalagmites. These ancient caves offer an unforgettable journey into the depths of the earth, showcasing spectacular geological formations.

The medieval fortress of Gradara stands as a testament to the region's rich history, its imposing walls and towers narrating tales of chivalry and romance. Explore the well-preserved castle and imagine the historical sagas that unfolded within its bounds.

In Loreto, marvel at the Basilica della Santa Casa, a sanctuary steeped in religious significance and artistic splendor. This pilgrimage site captivates with its stunning architecture and the revered Holy House, believed by many to be the home of the Virgin Mary.

The town of Recanati invites art and literature enthusiasts to walk in the footsteps of the great poet Giacomo Leopardi. Experience the town's lyrical charm and visit the Leopardi House Museum, a haven of literary heritage nestled amidst the picturesque landscape.

Discover the coastal allure of Sirolo and Numana, jewels of the Adriatic. These charming towns, set against the backdrop of the Conero Riviera, offer breathtaking sea views, enchanting beaches, and a serene escape from the bustle of city life.

Marche's vibrant culinary scene reflects its rich gastronomic heritage, with a focus on locally sourced ingredients and traditional recipes. Savor dishes like porchetta, vincisgrassi, and succulent seafood specialties along the coast.

Delve deeper into the heart of Marche's gastronomic culture, where the flavors of the land and sea are artfully blended in its local cuisine. This region, bountiful in its agricultural produce, offers a plethora of culinary delights that are a testament to its rich and varied gastronomic heritage. Savor the unique taste of Marche's wines, like the robust red Verdicchio and the fragrant white Lacrima di Morro d'Alba, which perfectly encapsulate the essence of the region's terroir.

Indulge in the region's cheese-making tradition with specialties such as the creamy and delicate Casciotta d'Urbino DOP, a cheese that has graced the tables since the Renaissance period, and the Pecorino dei Monti Sibillini, a sheep's milk cheese known for its rich flavor and texture. These cheeses not only add depth to the local cuisine but also embody the region's pastoral heritage.

The Marche culinary experience extends to its diverse array of traditional dishes, like the hearty Vincisgrassi, a lasagna richly layered with meat and béchamel, and Brodetto, a flavorful seafood stew that varies from coast to coast, each version reflecting the local catch and tradition. The region's olive oil, with its distinct flavors, adds a touch of culinary artistry to every dish.

As you journey through Marche, the combination of its exquisite wines, artisanal cheeses, and traditional culinary creations offer a symphony of tastes, an essential aspect of exploring the hidden beauty of this Italian region. Each meal in Marche is not just sustenance but a celebration of its land, a culinary adventure waiting to be savored.

Delve into the authentic charm of Marche's medieval towns. Urbino, a UNESCO World Heritage Site and the birthplace of Raphael, is a must-visit for art lovers. Wander through Urbino's cobblestone streets, and then explore the architectural wonders of towns like Ascoli Piceno and Macerata.

Participate in the region's local traditions and festivals to fully immerse yourself in the Marche experience. Join the lively carnival in Fano, witness the historical La Quintana horse race in Ascoli Piceno, and partake in olive harvests and truffle festivals.

Marche, with its authenticity and hidden gems like the Frasassi Caves and the historical richness of Gradara and Loreto, is a truly special destination for those seeking a unique and immersive travel experience.

3.4 Off-the-Beaten-Path in Lazio

In the very heart of Italy, where ancient history and modern vibrancy converge, lies the region of Lazio. Often overshadowed by the eternal allure of Rome, its capital, Lazio is a treasure trove of hidden gems, each offering a unique glimpse into the rich tapestry of Italian culture, history, and natural beauty. This journey through Lazio invites you to step off the well-trodden paths and discover the lesser-known wonders that lie just beyond the bustling streets of Rome.

Lazio is not just a region; it's a narrative of diverse landscapes and historical epochs, a place where medieval villages perch atop volcanic cliffs, serene lakes mirror the sky, and ancient ruins tell tales of a bygone era. From the mystical charm of Calcata to the thermal baths of Viterbo, the dying city of Civita di Bagnoregio, and the cultural riches of Tivoli, Lazio beckons the curious traveler to explore its hidden corners.

Join us as we venture through Lazio, where every town, every landscape, and every monument is a chapter in a story waiting to be told. Let us uncover the secrets of this enchanting region, from the romantic gardens of Ninfa to the tranquil shores of Lago di Bolsena, the monastic heritage of Subiaco, and the ancient legacies of Ostia Antica and the Etruscan cities. Welcome to a journey through Lazio, where the past and present blend seamlessly, offering a travel experience that is as authentic as it is unforgettable.

Lazio, the region that encompasses Rome and is known for its rich history and ancient ruins, also offers several off-the-beaten-path destinations for adventurous travelers. Beyond the bustling capital, the region is a tapestry of historic towns, natural wonders, and serene landscapes.

Discover the enchanting town of Calcata, just over an hour's drive north of Rome. Perched on a volcanic cliff, this medieval village offers a journey back in time with its narrow streets, artisan shops, and artistic flair. The panoramic views of the surrounding valleys add to Calcata's mystical allure.

Viterbo, with its well-preserved medieval quarter and natural thermal baths, beckons travelers seeking historical immersion and relaxation. The San Pellegrino district, a maze of cobblestone streets and ancient buildings, leads to the grandeur of the Papal Palace. A dip in the Terme dei Papi offers a blend of luxury and history.

Step into another era in Civita di Bagnoregio, the 'dying city.' This hilltop marvel, accessible only by a pedestrian bridge, is a testament to resilience against time and nature. Its isolation and unique architecture make it a photographer's paradise.

Explore Tivoli, a treasure trove of cultural heritage. The Renaissance splendor of Villa d'Este and the ancient grandiosity of Villa Adriana are a feast for the eyes and the soul, offering a glimpse into Italy's opulent past.

The Giardini di Ninfa, a romantic and picturesque garden, provide a dreamlike escape amidst medieval ruins, crystal-clear streams, and a myriad of flowers and plants. This enchanting garden is a living painting, captivating all who wander its paths.

Experience the serene beauty of Lago di Bolsena, Europe's largest volcanic lake. Surrounded by quaint towns and lush vineyards, the lake's crystal-clear waters invite leisurely exploration and relaxation. The enchanting town of Bolsena, with its medieval castle and lakeside promenades, is a highlight of the lake's allure.

In Viterbo's vicinity, the medieval charm of Sermoneta captures the essence of timeless Italy. Explore its imposing Caetani Castle, wander through narrow streets, and experience the town's rich history and culture.

Delve into the spiritual tranquility at the Abbazia di Fossanova, an exemplary Cistercian architecture nestled in a peaceful setting. Its historical significance and serene atmosphere provide a contemplative escape from the bustling world.

The Parco Nazionale del Circeo presents a natural sanctuary with diverse ecosystems, perfect for nature lovers and birdwatchers. This coastal reserve showcases the unspoiled beauty of Lazio's landscapes.

In Subiaco, immerse yourself in monastic history at the Monastery of San Benedetto and Santa Scolastica. These ancient monasteries offer a glimpse into the life and legacy of Saint Benedict amidst the scenic Aniene Valley.

The ancient port city of Ostia Antica reveals the intricacies of Roman life. Its well-preserved ruins and mosaics are as captivating as they are educational, providing an in-depth look at ancient Roman civilization.

Discover the Etruscan legacy in Tarquinia and Cerveteri, where ancient necropolises with intricate tombs offer a fascinating journey into a civilization that predates Rome.

Monte Cassino, a site of historical and religious significance, stands as a symbol of peace and resilience. The Abbey of Monte Cassino, perched atop the hill, is a pilgrimage site for those interested in World War II history and Benedictine spirituality.

Beyond its historical and natural wonders, Lazio is also a region celebrated for its rich culinary heritage, where the flavors of the land and sea merge to create dishes unique to this part of Italy. The region's wines, like the crisp white Frascati and the full-bodied Cesanese, embody the diversity of Lazio's vineyards, offering a delightful accompaniment to the local cuisine.

Lazio's cheese-making tradition is highlighted by specialties such as the Pecorino Romano, a hard, salty cheese known for its distinct flavor, and the milder Caciotta Romana, both integral to the regional diet. These cheeses not only add depth to many local dishes but also stand out on their own as examples of the region's dairy expertise.

The culinary journey through Lazio is incomplete without savoring its traditional dishes, such as the classic Pasta alla Carbonara and Amatriciana, both of which have their roots in the region. The cuisine also showcases a variety of local vegetables, meats, and seafood, reflecting the agricultural richness of the region. Sample the savory Porchetta, a seasoned and slow-roasted pork dish, and enjoy the fresh flavors of local seafood along the coast.

As you travel through Lazio, the combination of its exquisite wines, artisanal cheeses, and traditional culinary creations offer a symphony of tastes, an essential aspect of exploring the region's hidden beauty. Each meal in Lazio is not just a feast for the palate but a celebration of its land, a culinary adventure waiting to be savored.

Lazio, extending beyond the allure of Rome, invites travelers to its hidden gems and lesser-known treasures. From Calcata's artistic streets to Viterbo's thermal baths, and from Civita di Bagnoregio's dramatic perch to Tivoli's regal villas, the region offers a mosaic of experiences that capture the heart of central Italy's authentic charm. Whether wandering through the enchanting streets of Sermoneta, exploring the historical depths of Subiaco, or basking in the tranquility of the gardens of Ninfa, Lazio unfolds as a region rich with undiscovered stories and picturesque settings.

3.5 Delights of the Vatican City and Rome

In the midst of Rome, the eternal city that has stood as a witness to the march of history, lies the Vatican City, a sovereign enclave that encapsulates the essence of art, history, and spirituality. Despite its modest geographical footprint, the Vatican City is a colossal presence in the world of art, culture, and religion. This journey into the heart of the Vatican City and Rome is an exploration of a heritage that transcends time and borders, offering a window into the soul of Italy and the legacy of humanity.

The Vatican City, with its Vatican Museums, Sistine Chapel, and St. Peter's Basilica, is not just a destination; it's an odyssey through centuries of artistic and spiritual endeavors. It stands as a testament to the heights of human creativity and devotion, where every fresco, every sculpture, and every architectural detail tells a story of faith, genius, and beauty.

As we wander through the Vatican and the streets of Rome, we are walking through pages of history, where ancient ruins coexist with Renaissance masterpieces, and the whispers of the past meet the vitality of the present. Rome, with its Colosseum, Roman Forum, Pantheon, and countless other treasures, is a living museum, a celebration of life and art in all their forms.

Join us on this journey through the Vatican City and Rome, where every corner reveals a new marvel, every step is a journey through time, and every experience is a brushstroke on the canvas of cultural legacy. Let us embrace the awe-inspiring beauty of the Vatican and the timeless allure of Rome, and let these eternal cities inspire and enchant us with their stories, art, and soul. Welcome to a journey into the heart of Italy's artistic and spiritual heritage.

The Vatican City, situated within the borders of Rome, is the smallest independent state in the world. Despite its diminutive size, it holds immense cultural and historical significance, boasting a rich tapestry of artistic and spiritual treasures. At the heart of these is the Vatican Museums, a must-visit attraction where an extraordinary collection of art and artifacts accumulated by various popes throughout the centuries is displayed. As you wander through these halls, you'll encounter masterpieces by renowned artists like Michelangelo and Raphael, culminating in the awe-inspiring Sistine Chapel with its iconic ceiling frescoes painted by Michelangelo.

Explore the serene Vatican Gardens, a horticultural marvel offering a peaceful escape from the bustling city, with manicured lawns, intricate fountains, and an array of flora. The hidden Necropoli Vaticana beneath St. Peter's Basilica unveils a subterranean world of ancient tombs and relics, offering a unique glimpse into early Christian history.

St. Peter's Basilica, an architectural marvel and the largest church in the world, stands as a symbol of the grandeur and beauty of the Vatican. Its intricate mosaics, stunning sculptures, and the panoramic views from the dome are unmatched. The Vatican City also offers the unique opportunity to witness the mesmerizing Papal audience, a deeply spiritual experience where the Pope addresses and blesses the crowd.

Rome, the capital city of Italy, is a treasure trove of history, art, and culture. Beyond the iconic Colosseum and the magnificent Roman Forum, delve into the lesser-known yet captivating Quartiere Coppedè, a whimsical district showcasing an eclectic mix of architectural styles. The Pantheon, with its stunning dome, remains an architectural wonder, while the ancient Roman road of Via Appia Antica offers a tranquil stroll amidst historic ruins and natural beauty.

In the heart of Rome, the Chiesa di San Clemente, with its multi-layered history, is a hidden gem revealing layers of ancient temples and early Christian artifacts. The city's beauty extends to the Spanish Steps, the Trevi Fountain, and the Piazza Navona, each a showcase of Rome's artistic heritage.

The tranquil Parco degli Acquedotti, with its ancient aqueducts, offers a unique blend of historical grandeur and natural beauty. Indulge in authentic Italian cuisine at local trattorias and gelaterias, savoring traditional dishes like pasta carbonara and tiramisu.

Wander through the bustling streets to the Centrale Montemartini, where the contrast of classical art and industrial machinery creates an unexpected and striking setting. The Giardino degli Aranci, perched atop the Aventine Hill, provides a serene oasis with spectacular views of Rome.

Every corner of Rome and the Vatican City tells a story, from the hidden gardens and ancient tombs to the architectural marvels and secret corners. These destinations offer a unique opportunity to delve into the heart of Italian culture and history, leaving visitors with lasting memories of their time spent in these iconic places.

3.6 Lesser-Known Wonders of Abruzzo

In the heart of Italy, away from the well-worn paths of tourist itineraries, lies Abruzzo, a region that is a tapestry of natural beauty, historical richness, and cultural depth. This hidden gem, nestled between the Apennine Mountains and the Adriatic Sea, invites you on a journey through unspoiled landscapes, medieval villages, and a heritage that resonates with the authenticity of Italian life.

Abruzzo is not just a region; it's an exploration of Italy's untamed beauty and historical wealth. From the towering peaks of Gran Sasso d'Italia to the charming streets of Sulmona, the pristine wilderness of the Abruzzo National Park, and the medieval allure of Santo Stefano di Sessanio, every corner of Abruzzo tells a story of a land steeped in tradition and nature's artistry.

Join us on this journey through Abruzzo, where the tranquility of nature meets the echoes of the past. Let us discover the serene beauty of Lake Scanno, the ancient fortifications of Rocca Calascio, the archeological wonders of Chieti, and the picturesque Costa dei Trabocchi. Abruzzo offers a mosaic of experiences that beckon the traveler seeking something beyond the ordinary.

Welcome to a journey through Abruzzo, a region that promises not just breathtaking landscapes and historical discoveries, but also an intimate encounter with the heart and soul of central Italy. Let us venture into this hidden realm, where every path leads to discovery and every moment is a tribute to Italy's enduring charm.

Abruzzo, a region in central Italy, is often overlooked by tourists in favor of more well-known destinations. However, this hidden gem is home to a plethora of lesser-known wonders that are waiting to be explored. The Gran Sasso d'Italia, the highest peak in the Apennine Mountains, is a paradise for nature lovers and hikers. With its stunning landscapes and diverse flora and fauna, it offers a sense of tranquility and adventure.

The town of Sulmona, famous for its production of confetti, sugared almonds that are a traditional Italian wedding favor, captivates visitors with its picturesque streets. The Confetti Museum provides insight into this sweet tradition's history and craftsmanship.

Abruzzo National Park, spanning over 150,000 acres, is a must-visit for wildlife enthusiasts. Home to the rare Marsican brown bear, it offers unique wildlife spotting opportunities amidst beautiful natural scenery.

Santo Stefano di Sessanio, a well-preserved medieval village, offers a glimpse into the past with its narrow streets, stone houses, and ancient defensive walls. It provides breathtaking views of the surrounding countryside and a rich historical atmosphere.

Discover Scanno, a charming village renowned for its scenic lake and traditional silver filigree jewelry. The town's artisanal heritage and natural beauty make it a unique stop in the heart of Abruzzo.

Rocca Calascio, a medieval fortress set high in the mountains, offers spectacular views and a journey back in time. Its dramatic setting has made it a favorite location for filmmakers and a must-see for visitors.

In Chieti, explore the rich history and archeological treasures at the Museo Archeologico Nazionale d'Abruzzo, which houses significant artifacts of the Italic civilization.

Experience the beauty of the Costa dei Trabocchi, where ancient fishing structures dot the coastline. This area is known for its stunning sea views and fresh seafood, offering a unique culinary experience.

As you immerse yourself in the beauty of Abruzzo, let the region's culinary treasures guide your journey. Known for its diverse and hearty cuisine, Abruzzo offers a gastronomic experience that is as rich and varied as its landscapes. Taste the robust flavors of the local Montepulciano d'Abruzzo wine, a red that captures the essence of the region's vineyards, and the crisp and refreshing Trebbiano d'Abruzzo, perfect for accompanying a wide range of dishes.

Indulge in the region's cheese-making heritage with specialties like Pecorino d'Abruzzo, a sheep's milk cheese that is both sharp and savory, and Scamorza, a smoked cheese with a unique texture and flavor. These cheeses not only add depth to the culinary offerings but also reflect the pastoral traditions of the region.

The cuisine of Abruzzo is characterized by its simplicity and the use of locally sourced ingredients. Savor the flavors of traditional dishes such as 'Arrosticini', succulent skewers of lamb or mutton, and 'Maccheroni alla chitarra', a pasta dish often served with a hearty lamb ragu. The region is also known for its flavorful olive oils and truffles, adding a distinctive touch to many of its dishes.

As you explore the diverse landscapes and historic towns of Abruzzo, take the opportunity to dine in local trattorias where traditional recipes are lovingly prepared, offering an authentic taste of Abruzzese cuisine. Each meal in Abruzzo is not just a feast for the palate but a celebration of its rich agricultural and culinary heritage.

Abruzzo, with its diverse landscapes and historical gems, is a region that offers something for everyone. From the majestic Gran Sasso to the tranquil shores of the Costa dei Trabocchi, and from the historical streets of Sulmona to the medieval ambiance of Santo Stefano di Sessanio, it's a region rich with undiscovered stories and breathtaking sights. So, when planning your next trip to Italy, include Abruzzo in your itinerary and uncover the hidden gems that this remarkable region has to offer.

Chapter 4: Southern Italy's Hidden Gems

4.1 Lesser-Known Wonders of Sardinia

In the heart of the Mediterranean, where the sea's azure embrace meets an island of breathtaking beauty, lies Sardinia. This jewel of Southern Italy, with over 1,800 kilometers of stunning coastline, is more than just a beach paradise; it is a land rich in history, culture, and natural wonders. Sardinia's shores, from the glittering Costa Smeralda to the serene Gulf of Orosei and beyond, are a mosaic of unique treasures, each beach and cove telling its own enchanting story.

Sardinia is not just a destination; it is an experience, a journey through diverse landscapes and millennia of history. From the luxury and natural splendor of the Costa Smeralda to the dramatic cliffs and hidden beaches of the Gulf of Orosei, and from the historic towns like Alghero and Cagliari to the tranquil beauty of the inland regions, Sardinia invites you to discover its many facets.

Join us on this exploration of Sardinia, where every stretch of sand, every ancient ruin, and every winding street in its charming towns is a chapter in a story of mesmerizing beauty and rich heritage. Let us uncover the secrets of this island, from the unspoiled shores of Villasimius and Stintino to the historical richness of Chia and Bosa, and from the natural wonders of the Grotte di Nettuno to the wild beauty of the Parco Nazionale dell'Asinara.

Welcome to a journey through Sardinia, where the allure of the coast is matched only by the charm of its towns and the majesty of its mountains. Here, the past and present merge in a landscape that is as varied as it is beautiful, offering a travel experience that is as authentic as it is unforgettable. Welcome to the hidden splendor of Sardinia, a true Mediterranean paradise waiting to be explored.

With over 1,800 kilometers of captivating coastline, Sardinia stands as a beacon of beauty, home to some of the most pristine and unexplored beaches in the world. These shores are akin to glittering jewels, each beach a unique treasure, scattered along the shore like diamonds in the sun. The island's vast coastline is a tapestry of natural splendor, with each stretch of sand and sea telling its own mesmerizing story.

The renowned Costa Smeralda, a beacon of luxury and natural beauty, is famous for its sandy beaches that stretch out like ribbons of gold, and crystal-clear waters that dance with hues of deep blue and vibrant turquoise. The light here plays off the water, creating a spectacle of colors that is nothing short of hypnotic. It's a place where the sun kisses the sea, and the gentle breeze whispers tales of ancient mariners.

In contrast, the untouched beaches of the Gulf of Orosei offer a completely different kind of beauty. Here, the dramatic cliffs create a breathtaking backdrop to the serene beaches. Each cove and stretch of sand in this area is a hidden gem, offering breathtaking scenery and a sense of peace that is increasingly rare in our busy world. The Gulf of Orosei is a sanctuary where the rhythm of the waves dictates the pace of the day.

Moving inland, the coastal town of Alghero captivates visitors with its charming old town, steeped in history, and the imposing Catalan walls that speak of a rich, multicultural past. The town is a fusion of cultures, a place where every stone and street has a story to tell, from ancient times to the present day.

Cagliari, the island's capital, is a treasure trove of history and culture. This vibrant city is where tradition and modernity meet, creating a lively yet relaxed atmosphere. The streets of Cagliari are lined with historic buildings, each echoing the island's diverse history, from Roman ruins to medieval churches, blending seamlessly with contemporary life.

Further along the coast, Villasimius and Stintino are celebrated for their idyllic beaches and turquoise waters. Villasimius, with its panoramic views and marine reserve, is a paradise for those who seek tranquility as well as underwater adventure. Stintino's La Pelosa beach, with its fine white sand and shallow waters, is perfect for families and those looking to unwind in a picturesque setting.

In Chia, the tranquil beaches and rolling sand dunes offer a serene escape from the hustle and bustle of daily life. The sound of the waves here is like a soothing melody, lulling visitors into a state of peaceful relaxation. Meanwhile, the picturesque river town of Bosa enchants visitors with its colorful houses, vibrant riverfront, and the warmth of its local community. This charming town, with its cobbled streets and authentic Sardinian ambiance, is a delightful discovery for those exploring the island.

Yet, the wonders of Sardinia are not confined to its coastline. The island is a mosaic of astonishing natural attractions. The Grotte di Nettuno, accessible by sea or via the dramatic Escala del Cabirol staircase, is a marvel of nature's architecture. These caverns, with their stalactites and stalagmites, create an otherworldly experience, transporting visitors to a time when the earth was still crafting its masterpieces.

The Parco Nazionale dell'Asinara, a protected island, is a haven of biodiversity. It is home to a rich array of wildlife, including the famous albino donkeys, which roam freely in this unspoiled natural paradise. For trekking and nature enthusiasts, the rugged landscapes of Supramonte and the deep canyons of Gola di Gorropu offer unparalleled adventures. These areas are a testament to the island's geologic past, offering challenging trails and breathtaking views.

The Archipelago della Maddalena, known for its crystal-clear waters, is a mesmerizing cluster of islands, each with its own unique beauty and story. These islands are a paradise for sailors, divers, and nature lovers, offering some of the most stunning seascapes in the Mediterranean.

Sardinia's rich tapestry of history is evident in its archaeological sites. The UNESCO World Heritage site Nuraghe Su Nuraxi in Barumini is an extraordinary example of the Nuragic culture, showcasing the ingenuity of the island's ancient inhabitants. The ancient Phoenician and Roman site of Tharros offers a glimpse into the island's storied past, where civilizations converged and left their mark. The Punic-Roman necropolis of Tuvixeddu in Cagliari and the well-preserved sacred well at the Nuragic complex of Santa Cristina are portals to an ancient world, offering insights into the rituals and daily lives of past societies.

The soul of Sardinia is also captured in its rich culture and gastronomy. Orgosolo, with its vibrant murals, tells stories of the island's social and political history, while the National Archaeological Museum in Cagliari invites visitors to delve deeper into Sardinia's layered past. The island's culinary offerings are a feast for the senses, with local wine tastings featuring varietals like Cannonau and Vermentino, and traditional dishes like Porceddu, Culurgiones, and Pecorino Sardo showcasing the island's rich culinary heritage.

For those seeking adventure, Sardinia offers exhilarating activities. The windswept shores of Porto Pollo are a haven for windsurfing and kitesurfing enthusiasts, while the rugged terrain of the Gennargentu National Park presents challenging trekking opportunities. The island's crystal-clear beaches are perfect for snorkeling and diving, offering a glimpse into the vibrant underwater world.

In the heart of Sardinia, let the island's culinary treasures add another layer to your journey. The island is renowned for its distinctive and flavorful cuisine, deeply rooted in local traditions and the natural bounty of both land and sea. Indulge in the unique flavors of Sardinian wines, including the robust Cannonau, a red wine rich in aroma and body, and the crisp, refreshing Vermentino, a white wine that perfectly complements the island's seafood.

The cheese-making tradition in Sardinia is an art form, with varieties like Pecorino Sardo and Fiore Sardo offering a taste of the island's pastoral heritage. These sheep's milk cheeses are known for their rich flavors and are a staple in Sardinian cuisine.

Sardinian cuisine is characterized by its simplicity and the use of fresh, locally sourced ingredients. Experience the authenticity of dishes such as Porceddu, a succulent spit-roasted suckling pig, and Culurgiones, a type of stuffed pasta that is a regional specialty. The island's coastal areas provide a bounty of fresh seafood, which is expertly prepared in traditional dishes that reflect the island's rich maritime heritage.

As you travel across Sardinia, take the opportunity to dine in local agriturismos and trattorias where you can enjoy traditional recipes handed down through generations. Here, meals are more than just food; they are a celebration of Sardinian culture and a testament to the island's rich agricultural and culinary history.

Sardinia is a land of contrasts and surprises, offering something for every traveler. Whether you're a sun seeker, an adventurer, or a culture enthusiast, the island's myriad attractions, from its coastal jewels to its inland treasures, have something for everyone. Its untouched beauty, rich history, and diverse attractions make it a dream destination for those seeking an escape from the crowds and a chance to connect with both nature and the soul of this remarkable island. Discover the hidden splendor of Southern Italy and experience the allure of Sardinia's captivating treasures, a true Mediterranean paradise.

4.2 Discovering the Charm of Campania

In the sun-kissed south of Italy, where the Tyrrhenian Sea laps against a land steeped in history and culture, lies Campania. This enchanting region, often overshadowed by the allure of its capital city, Naples, is a tapestry of hidden wonders and breathtaking landscapes, each thread weaving a story of the past and present. Campania is not just a region; it is a journey through time, where ancient ruins, lush landscapes, and vibrant towns come together in a symphony of Italian splendor.

From the historic streets of Naples to the regal beauty of the Reggia di Caserta, the captivating island of Capri, and the picturesque Amalfi Coast, Campania beckons the traveler to explore its many facets. The region is a mosaic of experiences, offering a blend of natural beauty, rich history, and cultural depth.

Join us as we traverse Campania, where every corner reveals a new marvel, every path leads to discovery, and every experience is a brushstroke on the canvas of Italian heritage. Let us uncover the secrets of this enchanting region, from the untouched beaches of the Cilento area to the ancient splendors of Paestum and Velia, and from the serene landscapes of the national park to the traditional flavors of its cuisine.

Welcome to a journey through Campania, where the echoes of history meet the vibrancy of the present, offering a travel experience that is as authentic as it is unforgettable. Let us embark on this exploration of Italy's hidden gem, where the heart and soul of the south are waiting to be discovered.

Campania, a region steeped in the allure of southern Italy, unfolds as a narrative rich in history, culture, and breathtaking landscapes. This hidden gem, with its tapestry of picturesque towns and ancient ruins, is a testament to Italy's enduring charm and mystique.

Naples, the vibrant heart of Campania, is a city where the echoes of history resonate through bustling streets. The city's lifeblood is its rich heritage, evident in landmarks like the Naples National Archaeological Museum. This museum is not just a repository of artifacts; it's a journey through time, where each relic tells a story of civilizations long past. In the same city, the Royal Palace of Naples stands as a proud reminder of regal grandeur, its majestic halls whispering tales of the Savoy dynasty's opulence.

Beyond the urban landscape, the island of Capri emerges from the

Tyrrhenian Sea like a siren's call. Capri is a blend of natural wonders and luxurious escapism, where the rugged cliffs meet the serenity of the sea. The island's famed Grotta Azzurra, a marvel of nature's artistry, offers an otherworldly experience as light and water dance in a captivating azure ballet.

The Amalfi Coast, a ribbon of coastal beauty, weaves its way through the region. Towns like Positano, Amalfi, and Ravello are perched precariously on cliffs, their colorful facades a testament to Italian charm. The Amalfi Coast is more than just a scenic journey; it's an immersive experience where the Mediterranean lifestyle can be savored in every limoncello sip and every sun-soaked vista.

Pompeii and Herculaneum, frozen in time by the wrath of Vesuvius, offer an unparalleled glimpse into ancient Roman life. These archaeological sites are not mere tourist destinations; they are portals to a bygone era, where the streets, homes, and public squares tell a story of daily life, culture, and tragedy.

Yet, Campania's narrative extends beyond these renowned locales. The Reggia di Caserta, often overlooked, is a jewel in the region's crown. This 18th-century royal palace is a masterpiece of Baroque art and architecture, its grandiose design and sprawling gardens rivaling the palaces of Europe's greatest monarchs.

The Toledo Metro Station in Naples, a subterranean wonder, is a contemporary art display, transforming a public space into a canvas of creativity and design. Casa Vanvitelliana in Bacoli and the Sansevero Chapel Museum in Naples reveal the artistic soul of Campania, each location offering unique insights into the region's artistic legacy.

In the cuisine of Campania, the story of the land and sea is told. Dishes such as swordfish involtini and the fiery 'nduja are culinary expressions of the region's bounty. The wines of Campania, including the celebrated Falanghina and Greco di Tufo, are liquid narratives of the region's rich viticultural history.

In the southern reaches of Campania lies the Cilento area, a less trodden but equally mesmerizing part of the region. The Cilento and Vallo di Diano National Park, a UNESCO World Heritage site, is a mosaic of diverse landscapes, from rugged mountains to serene coastal lines, embodying the untouched beauty of nature. This sprawling natural sanctuary is a haven for hikers, history enthusiasts, and anyone seeking to escape into the serenity of nature.

Cilento's charm extends beyond its natural beauty. The area is steeped in history and tradition, evident in its ancient ruins and quaint, timeless villages. Paestum, within Cilento, stands as a proud reminder of Magna Graecia's grandeur, its well-preserved Greek temples narrating tales of ancient glory. The towns in Cilento, such as Agropoli and Castellabate, offer a glimpse into traditional Italian life, their narrow streets and historic buildings echoing centuries of stories.

The culinary journey through Cilento is as enchanting as its landscapes. The region is known for its unique flavors, with dishes like 'Cilento Figs' and 'White Artichokes' highlighting the local produce. The region's olive oil, marked by its distinct taste, is a product of the ancient olive groves that dot the landscape. The local wines, embodying the essence of the region's terroir, complement the gastronomic experience, offering a taste of Cilento's rich agricultural heritage.

In Cilento, every path leads to discovery, whether it's exploring the majestic ruins of Velia, an ancient city of philosophical renown, or wandering through the picturesque streets of its coastal towns. The area's beaches, some of the most pristine in Italy, offer a tranquil retreat from the bustling tourist spots, their crystal-clear waters inviting relaxation and reflection.

Cilento, though less renowned than its northern neighbors, is a region that captivates with its authenticity and unspoiled beauty. It is a place where the heartbeat of old Italy is still felt, where nature, history, and tradition blend seamlessly to create an experience that is both deeply rooted and transcendent. A journey through Cilento is a journey into the soul of southern Italy, a chapter in the Campanian narrative that is as rich and captivating as any other.

Campania, with its sun-drenched landscapes and rich soils, is a paradise for food and wine enthusiasts. This region's culinary journey is as diverse as its landscapes, offering flavors that capture the essence of Southern Italian gastronomy. Indulge in the famous Neapolitan pizza, a culinary icon with its soft, chewy crust and rich toppings, perfected in the bustling streets of

Naples. Savor the traditional 'Spaghetti alle Vongole,' a simple yet flavorful dish that brings the taste of the sea to your plate.

Campania's cheese-making tradition shines in the form of Mozzarella di Bufala Campana DOP, a soft, creamy delight made from the milk of water buffaloes. This cheese is a staple in the region's cuisine, known for its freshness and quality.

The region's wines are a reflection of its varied terroir, from the volcanic soils of Vesuvius to the coastal breezes of the Amalfi Coast. Explore the rich flavors of Taurasi, a bold red wine with deep complexity, and Falanghina, a crisp white wine that encapsulates the region's sun-kissed vineyards. The lesser-known but equally delightful Lacryma Christi, produced on the slopes of Mount Vesuvius, is a testament to the region's unique winemaking history.

Campania's culinary landscape is further enriched by its seafood delicacies, particularly along the Amalfi Coast. Here, dishes such as 'Scialatielli ai Frutti di Mare' and 'Pesce all'Acqua Pazza' showcase the region's mastery in seafood preparation, blending fresh ingredients with traditional cooking techniques.

In the heart of Campania, the fertile lands give rise to a variety of fresh produce, including San Marzano tomatoes, celebrated for their rich flavor and used extensively in local dishes. The region's olive oil, with its distinct fruity notes, adds another layer of flavor to its culinary creations.

As you journey through Campania, be sure to visit local trattorias and vineyards, where you can experience the region's gastronomic diversity firsthand. These culinary experiences are not just about tasting; they are about immersing yourself in the culture and tradition that define Campania's rich food and wine heritage.

Campania is a region where every town, every landscape, and every flavor tells a part of its story. From the historic streets of Naples to the royal elegance of the Reggia di Caserta, the enchanting island of Capri, and the picturesque Amalfi Coast, each destination is a chapter in a larger tale. This region invites travelers to embark on a journey of discovery, to experience the wonder of Italy's hidden gem, where history, culture, and beauty converge in a timeless dance.

4.3 Hidden Cultural Gems of Molise

Nestled in the rolling hills of Molise, a region often overshadowed by its more famous Italian neighbors, lies the ancient town of Sepino, or Saepinum as it was known in its Roman heyday. This hidden gem, rich in history and culture, is a portal to a bygone era, offering a glimpse into the life and times of the ancient Romans. Sepino, with its remarkably preserved archaeological site, invites visitors on a journey back in time, to walk the streets once trodden by Roman citizens and to marvel at the remnants of a once-thriving city.

Sepino is not just an archaeological site; it's a story etched in stone, a testament to the grandeur and sophistication of the Roman Empire. From the majestic Roman theater, a symbol of ancient entertainment and artistry, to the amphitheater, where the echoes of gladiatorial battles still seem to resonate, Sepino captivates the imagination and ignites a passion for history.

Join us on this exploration of Sepino, where every ruin, every stone, and every path tells a part of the story of ancient Rome's influence in Molise. Let us wander through the remains of the forum, the beating heart of Saepinum, where the hustle and bustle of daily life once played out, and let us imagine the lives of the people who called this place home.

Welcome to a journey through Sepino, a hidden treasure in Molise, where the past and present merge, offering a unique opportunity to step off the beaten path and immerse oneself in the rich tapestry of Italy's ancient history. Let us discover the beauty and mystery of this lesser-known but equally enchanting corner of Italy.

Sepino, formerly known as Saepinum, was once a bustling ancient Roman city that thrived in the heart of Molise. Today, this remarkable town offers visitors the opportunity to step back in time and explore its remarkably preserved archaeological site. As you wander through the ancient streets of Sepino, you can't help but be captivated by the remnants of its glorious past.

The highlight of the Sepino archaeological site is the Roman theater, a testament to the grandeur and sophistication of ancient Roman entertainment. Imagine yourself sitting among the spectators, listening to the echoes of applause as actors performed captivating plays and comedies on the stage. The theater's architecture, although partially ruined, still exudes an aura of elegance and grandiosity.

Adjacent to the theater, you'll find the remains of an amphitheater, where fierce gladiatorial battles once took place. Stand in the center of the arena and let your imagination run wild as you envision the roaring crowds, the clash of swords, and the adrenaline-fueled excitement that permeated the air. The amphitheater's crumbling walls hint at the thrilling spectacles that unfolded within its confines.

Continuing your journey through Sepino's archaeological site, you'll stumble upon the remnants of a forum, the bustling center of civic and commercial life in ancient Roman cities. Picture the market stalls, the lively conversations, and the political debates that animated this vibrant hub. Even in its current state of decay, the forum evokes a sense of community and serves as a reminder of the rich social fabric that once thrived in Sepino.

Exploring Sepino's archaeological site is not just a journey through ancient history; it is an opportunity to gain insight into the daily lives of the Romans. As you walk amidst the ruins, imagine the footsteps of citizens going about their daily routines, the aroma of food wafting from nearby taverns, and the echoes of conversations that filled the air. In Sepino, time seems to stand still, allowing visitors to immerse themselves in a bygone era.

In Molise, with its rolling hills and rich history, the culinary heritage is not just a footnote but a significant chapter in its story. Here, in the town of Sepino and its surrounding countryside, ancient Roman culinary traditions blend with quintessentially Italian flavors, creating a unique gastronomic experience. The local recipes, passed down through generations, offer an authentic taste of Molise's flavors.

A cornerstone of Molise's cuisine is its cheese. The Caciocavallo of Agnone, a stretched-curd cheese produced exclusively in Molise, is a fine example of the region's dairy heritage. With its smooth texture and rich flavor, this cheese is a must-try for any cheese aficionado visiting Sepino.

The wines of Molise, though less known compared to other Italian regions, are hidden gems in their own right. Varieties like Tintilia, a rich and full-bodied red, and Biferno, a blend of local grape varieties, reflect the unique terroir and the passion of Molise's winemakers. A visit to local wineries offers a chance to taste these exclusive wines, pairing them with traditional dishes of the area.

The cuisine of Sepino and Molise as a whole is marked by simple yet flavorful dishes. Specialties like 'Pampanella', a spiced and slow-cooked pork roast, and 'Pasta e Fagioli con le Cotiche', a comforting dish of pasta and beans with pork rind, showcase how the local cuisine celebrates earth's bounty.

In Sepino, a complete culinary experience involves tasting the local olive oils. The extra virgin olive oil from Molise, with its fruity flavor and slightly spicy finish, is perfect for dressing salads or to accompany a piece of fresh bread.

Visit Sepino and Molise not just for its archaeological treasures, but also to delight your palate with local delicacies. In this region, each dish tells a story, each glass of wine is a journey through the land's traditions, and every taste is an indelible memory of Molise's culinary charm.

Visiting Sepino in Molise is like unearthing a hidden treasure. It is an invitation to delve into a lesser-known but equally captivating part of Italy's historical tapestry. So, take a step off the beaten path, and let Sepino's archaeological wonders transport you back in time to a world where the Romans reigned supreme and left an indelible mark on the landscape of Molise.

4.4 Unveiling the Mysteries of Puglia

In the sun-drenched heel of Italy's boot lies Puglia, a region rich in history, culture, and natural beauty. Often referred to as Apulia in English, this enchanting region is a mosaic of picturesque landscapes, charming towns, and ancient traditions, making it an undiscovered jewel in the crown of Southern Italy.

Puglia is not just a destination; it's an experience, a journey through a land where the past and present coexist in beautiful harmony. From the whimsical trulli houses of Alberobello to the Baroque grandeur of Lecce, and from the mystic caves of Castellana to the rugged beauty of the Gargano Peninsula, Puglia beckons the traveler to explore its many facets.

Join us on this exploration of Puglia, where every town, every landscape, and every dish tells a story of a land steeped in history and brimming with beauty.

Let us uncover the secrets of this enchanting region, from the serene coastlines of Polignano a Mare and Monopoli to the historic allure of Ostuni and the culinary delights of the Salento area.

Welcome to a journey through Puglia, where the allure of the coast is matched only by the charm of its towns and the richness of its cultural heritage. Here, the heart and soul of Southern Italy are waiting to be discovered, offering a travel experience that is as authentic as it is unforgettable. Welcome to the hidden splendor of Puglia, a true Mediterranean paradise waiting to be explored.

Welcome to the captivating region of Puglia, a treasure trove of hidden wonders in southern Italy. Known to the English-speaking world as Apulia, this region beckons with an authentic Italian experience, richly woven with history, culture, and breathtaking natural beauty.

Your journey begins in Alberobello, a fairy-tale town where the unique trulli houses, with their iconic conical roofs, stand as symbols of traditional Apulian architecture. These enchanting structures create a magical ambiance, transporting visitors to a bygone era, and offering a glimpse into the ingenious building techniques of the past.

In Lecce, often hailed as the 'Florence of the South,' you'll be mesmerized by the city's ornate Baroque architecture. The Chiesa di Santa Croce is a masterpiece of design, while the ancient Roman ruins, like the Anfiteatro Romano, are a testament to the city's rich historical tapestry. Lecce's elegance is further accentuated by its dynamic street life and a culinary scene that tantalizes the senses with local flavors.

Venture into the subterranean world of the Grotte di Castellana, a labyrinth of awe-inspiring caves adorned with stalactite and stalagmite formations. This underground wonderland reveals the artistic hand of nature, sculpting over millennia to create a mystical realm beneath the earth.

Polignano a Mare, perched atop limestone cliffs overlooking the Adriatic Sea, offers breathtaking vistas and a glimpse into old-world charm. This coastal gem is the epitome of the Apulian lifestyle, where one can indulge in fresh seafood while soaking in the stunning seascape.

As you meander through the Valle d'Itria, you'll be enchanted by a verdant tapestry interspersed with trulli and ancient masserie. This valley is the heartland of Puglia's agricultural abundance, where the earth yields exquisite olive oil and wines that are a testament to the region's fertile lands.

In Ostuni, the 'White City,' wander through sun-kissed, whitewashed streets, offering panoramic views over olive groves that stretch to the azure sea. This city is a photographer's dream, where the play of light and shadow brings to life the intricate details of its architecture.

The Salento area, the heel of Italy's boot, is a cultural mosaic where pristine beaches meet a tradition-rich land. Here, music, dance, and a cuisine that marries the riches of the sea with the fruits of the land create a sensory celebration.

Trani, a seaside town, enchants with its beautiful harbor and the magnificent Cattedrale di Santa Maria Assunta. This cathedral, standing regally by the sea, is a harmonious blend of sacred art and maritime heritage, capturing the soul of Puglia.

In Otranto, the easternmost tip of Italy, the imposing castle, crystal-clear waters, and the ancient mosaic floor of the Cathedral weave tales of medieval legends and lore, inviting visitors to step into a storybook setting.

Gallipoli, with its old town nestled on a limestone island, connected to the mainland by a historic bridge, offers a unique blend of beaches, vibrant nightlife, and historical allure. It's a place where relaxation and discovery go hand in hand.

Taranto, known as the city of two seas, marries its ancient Spartan heritage with a lively maritime present. The Aragonese Castle and the Spartan Museum are gateways into a history that spans thousands of years, telling tales of civilizations long past.

Bari, the pulsating capital of Puglia, is a city of contrasts. Here, the historic old town, the majestic Cattedrale di San Nicola, and the imposing Castello Normanno-Svevo stand alongside vibrant streets where traditional orecchiette pasta makers craft their wares and lively markets bustle with local life.

Venture to the northern reaches of Puglia, where Vieste and the Parco

Nazionale del Gargano offer rugged coastlines, ancient forests, and a sanctuary for wildlife. This region is an adventurer's paradise, a place where the natural world remains untamed and captivating.

The imposing Castel del Monte, a UNESCO World Heritage Site, fascinates with its unique octagonal design and mysterious origins. This 13th-century fortress, a masterpiece of medieval architecture, stands as a testament to the ingenuity and artistic vision of its creators.

In Monopoli, a coastal gem, the harmony of a picturesque harbor meets the allure of a rich historical center. It's a town that invites leisurely exploration and epitomizes the essence of seaside living.

The towns of Martina Franca and Cisternino, nestled in the picturesque Itria Valley, are architectural wonders. Their Baroque and Rococo facades, elegant palaces, and vibrant piazzas capture the spirit and charm of Puglia.

Fasano offers a unique blend of cultural exploration and wildlife adventure. Here, you can wander through the traditional town and delve into the wild at the Zoo Safari, offering an immersive experience into the animal kingdom.

At the southernmost point, Santa Maria di Leuca, where the Adriatic meets the Ionian Sea, stands as a panoramic wonder. Known for its historic lighthouse and sanctuary, it offers vistas where the waters of two seas blend under the Mediterranean sun.

Monte Sant'Angelo and the Santuario di San Michele Arcangelo, nestled in the Gargano heights, are not just pilgrimage sites but also vantage points offering awe-inspiring views of the surrounding landscapes. These sites resonate with spiritual and historical significance.

Discover Specchia, a hidden village that ranks among Italy's most beautiful. This hamlet is a maze of narrow streets and whitewashed houses, embodying the tranquil beauty of rural Puglia.

The Parco Nazionale dell'Alta Murgia and the Riserva Naturale di Torre Guaceto are bastions of unspoiled nature. These reserves offer peaceful retreats from the lively coastal towns, where the tranquility of nature reigns supreme.

Puglia, however, is not just a visual feast but a paradise for gourmets and food lovers. The region's cuisine is a journey through flavors and traditions, celebrating the land's bounty in every dish. Seafood here is transformed into culinary masterpieces, with dishes like grilled sea bass, cuttlefish, and frutti di mare offering a taste of the ocean's richness.

The rolling hills and fertile plains of Puglia are an agricultural haven. Ancient olive trees, their gnarled trunks a testament to centuries of cultivation, produce an olive oil that is a staple of local cuisine, enriching dishes with its rich, fruity essence.

The vineyards of Puglia, bathed in Mediterranean sun, are proud of their indigenous grape varieties. Negroamaro and Primitivo wines embody the essence of Puglia, full-bodied and rich, a reflection of the sun-drenched land from which they hail.

The culinary journey in Puglia takes you through a mosaic of flavors, from the humble yet delicious orecchiette con cime di rapa to the crunchy taralli, a perfect pairing with a glass of local wine. Each meal is a celebration, an opportunity to savor the agricultural heritage and culinary artistry of the region.

In Puglia, where history and culture intertwine with the landscape, the culinary journey is an essential part of the exploration. This sun-drenched region, known for its abundant harvests and traditional cooking, offers an array of gastronomic delights that embody the spirit of Southern Italy.

At the heart of Puglia's culinary heritage is its olive oil, renowned for its quality and flavor. The ancient olive groves of Puglia, some of the oldest in Italy, produce a golden elixir that is a staple in local kitchens, enriching dishes with its fruity and robust taste.

The region's cheese-making tradition is another facet of its rich culinary tapestry. Burrata, a creamy and delicate cheese, originated in Andria. This luscious cheese, with its soft exterior and rich, buttery center, is a delicacy that no visitor should miss. Similarly, the Canestrato Pugliese, a hard sheep's cheese, offers a sharp and tangy flavor that reflects the pastoral heritage of the region.

Puglia's vineyards yield wines that are as sun-kissed as the land itself. The

Primitivo di Manduria, a robust and fruity red, and the Negroamaro, known for its deep color and rich taste, are testament to the region's viticultural prowess. A visit to the vineyards and wineries of Puglia is not just a tasting experience but a journey through the history and culture of winemaking in the region.

The cuisine of Puglia is a celebration of simple yet flavorful ingredients. Dishes like orecchiette con cime di rapa, a pasta dish made with turnip greens, and tiella, a baked rice, potato, and mussel dish, showcase the region's ability to turn humble ingredients into culinary masterpieces.

In coastal towns like Polignano a Mare and Monopoli, the seafood is as fresh as the sea breeze. From grilled octopus to sea urchin pasta, the seafood dishes of Puglia are a testament to the region's close relationship with the Adriatic and Ionian seas.

Puglia's culinary scene is a journey in itself, a narrative told through flavors and aromas. Whether savoring a dish of freshly made pasta, enjoying a slice of creamy burrata, or sipping on a glass of rich Primitivo, every meal in Puglia is an invitation to indulge in the region's gastronomic heritage. Here, every bite tells a story of the land, the sea, and the people who have shaped this enchanting region.

As you traverse the landscapes of Puglia, from the Gargano Peninsula to the Salento area, let the local flavors guide your journey. Discover the hidden gems of Puglian cuisine, and experience the joy of dining where every meal is a celebration of life, tradition, and the bountiful harvests of this sun-kissed region.

Puglia, a symphony of natural beauty, historical richness, and culinary vibrancy, invites you to lose yourself in its enchanting towns, stunning landscapes, and the warmth of its people. Discover the hidden gems of this remarkable region and create memories that will linger long after your journey through southern Italy's hidden paradise.

4.5 Exploring the Authenticity of Basilicata

In the southern heart of Italy, where time moves to the rhythm of traditions and nature's beauty is etched into the landscape, lies Basilicata. This hidden gem, nestled between the more frequented regions of Puglia and Calabria, is a journey into an Italy untouched by mass tourism, a land where authenticity and simplicity are the true treasures.

Basilicata is not just a region; it's a testament to the enduring Italian spirit, a canvas where every hill, every ancient town, and every stretch of coastline tells a story. From the awe-inspiring Sassi di Matera to the vast expanses of the Pollino National Park, and from the picturesque villages of Castelmezzano and Pietrapertosa to the serene beauty of Maratea, Basilicata invites you to discover its hidden wonders.

Join us on this exploration of Basilicata, where history is carved into the landscape and culture is woven into the fabric of daily life. Let us uncover the secrets of this enchanting region, from the volcanic lakes and historic towns to the vibrant festivals that celebrate the rich tapestry of local customs and traditions.

Welcome to a journey through Basilicata, where the allure of the past meets the charm of the present, offering a travel experience that is as authentic as it is unforgettable. Let us embark on this discovery of Italy's hidden gem, where the beauty of simplicity and the richness of heritage create a symphony of experiences waiting to be explored. Welcome to the unspoiled splendor of Basilicata, a true testament to the timeless appeal of Southern Italy.

Basilicata, a region in southern Italy, often bypassed by tourists for busier destinations like Rome or Florence, is a treasure trove of authenticity and unexplored splendors. Nestled between Puglia and Calabria, Basilicata is a testament to the traditional Italian way of life, far from the paths of mass tourism.

This region is a canvas of breathtaking landscapes ranging from the rolling hills, rich with olive groves, to the rugged mountains and dramatic coastlines. The charm of Basilicata is further amplified by its picturesque hilltop towns and rich cultural tapestry.

A jewel in Basilicata's crown is the Sassi di Matera, a UNESCO World Heritage site. These ancient cave dwellings, sculpted from the rock, hark back to millennia and offer an extraordinary glimpse into human history. A stroll through Matera's Sassi is a journey back in time, where every alleyway and corner tells a story of resilience and ingenuity.

Not to be missed is the Parco Nazionale del Pollino, Italy's largest national park, a sanctuary for nature lovers and adventurers alike. Its diverse landscapes offer a backdrop for a variety of outdoor activities, from hiking to discovering rare flora and fauna.

The twin villages of Castelmezzano and Pietrapertosa, set against the stunning backdrop of the Dolomiti Lucane, present an awe-inspiring sight. Their unique location and the thrilling 'Volo dell'Angelo' zip-line attract thrill-seekers and photographers.

Maratea, the 'Pearl of the Tyrrhenian,' captivates visitors with its picturesque beaches and the striking Christ the Redeemer statue. Its coastal charm is complemented by a vibrant historical center, making it a perfect blend of beach relaxation and cultural exploration.

The serene beauty of Lago di Monticchio, encircled by lush forests and ancient monasteries, offers a peaceful retreat. Its volcanic origins add to the mystique, inviting visitors to enjoy nature walks and picnics by the water.

Venosa, a town steeped in history, showcases an array of Roman and medieval remains. The Incompiuta abbey and the imposing Castle of Pirro del Balzo are significant landmarks that narrate the town's rich past.

Basilicata's vibrant cultural heritage is celebrated through various festivals and events, reflecting the locals' pride in their traditions and customs. These festivities, from Easter processions to folk music festivals, are vibrant expressions of regional identity.

The culinary landscape of Basilicata is as rich as its history. Local dishes like 'peperoni cruschi' (crispy peppers), 'lucanica' sausage, and 'orecchiette' pasta with turnip greens are a testament to the region's agricultural bounty. The local markets bustle with activity, offering an array of fresh produce and authentic culinary experiences.

In the heart of Southern Italy, Basilicata emerges as a culinary paradise, where each dish and every sip of wine tells a story of the region's rich agricultural heritage and traditional cooking methods. This unexplored gem offers a gastronomic journey that complements its scenic beauty and historical richness.

Basilicata's cuisine is a reflection of its varied landscapes, from the rugged mountains to the fertile valleys. The region is famed for its Peperoni di Senise IGP, dried and crushed to create the unique 'peperoni cruschi,' a crunchy delicacy that adds flavor and texture to numerous traditional dishes.

In the realm of cheeses, Basilicata boasts the Pecorino di Filiano DOP, a sheep's milk cheese known for its rich and complex flavors, developed through careful aging processes. This cheese is not just a staple on the local tables but also a testament to the region's pastoral traditions.

The wine culture in Basilicata is epitomized by the Aglianico del Vulture DOC, a robust red wine derived from the Aglianico grape, grown in the volcanic soils around Mount Vulture. This wine, with its deep flavors and rich aroma, is a celebration of Basilicata's volcanic heritage and winemaking prowess.

Basilicata's culinary journey extends to its bread-making tradition, with Pane di Matera IGP being a notable example. This bread, with its distinctive shape and flavor, is baked using traditional methods, embodying the simplicity and authenticity of the region's food culture.

The region's pasta dishes, such as 'orecchiette con peperoni cruschi' and 'strascinati,' showcase the versatility of local ingredients. These pasta varieties, often handmade, are a staple in Basilicatan cuisine, served with hearty sauces that capture the essence of the region's flavors.

Lucanica, a traditional pork sausage, is a testament to the region's meat processing and preservation skills. Seasoned with local herbs and spices, this sausage is a key ingredient in many local dishes, offering a taste of Basilicata's culinary heritage.

Basilicata's cuisine is also characterized by its use of wild herbs and vegetables, such as 'rapa verde' and 'cardoncelli' mushrooms, which add unique flavors to the region's culinary palette. These ingredients, foraged from the wild or grown in local gardens, are a testament to the deep connection between the Basilicatan people and their land.

The region's sweets and desserts, such as 'calzoncelli' and 'torta di grano' (wheat cake), are a blend of simple ingredients and traditional recipes, offering a glimpse into Basilicata's festive and celebratory customs.

In Basilicata, every meal is an opportunity to explore the region's gastronomic diversity. From the robust flavors of its cheeses and wines to the simple yet satisfying taste of its traditional bread and pasta dishes, the region's cuisine is a journey through its agricultural past and present.

As you explore the scenic landscapes and historic towns of Basilicata, let your palate guide you through a culinary exploration that is as enriching as it is delicious. Experience the authentic flavors of this hidden Italian gem, where each dish is a celebration of the region's rich culinary traditions and bountiful harvests.

Basilicata, with its alluring landscapes, historical richness, and cultural vibrancy, is a destination that promises an authentic Italian experience. Its unspoiled beauty and charm make it an ideal choice for those seeking to explore Italy's hidden gems.

4.6 Hidden Gems of Calabria

In the sun-kissed toe of Italy's boot lies Calabria, a region steeped in history, culture, and natural beauty. Often bypassed by tourists in favor of more well-known Italian destinations, Calabria is a land of hidden gems and unexplored treasures, where the charm of southern Italy is manifested in its fullest glory.

Calabria is not just a destination; it's an experience, a journey through a land where the azure waters of the Tyrrhenian and Ionian Seas embrace rugged mountains and ancient ruins. From the breathtaking cliffside town of Tropea to the serene fishing village of Scilla, and from the historical allure of Rocca Imperiale to the natural splendor of the Sila National Park, Calabria beckons the traveler to discover its many facets.

Join us on this exploration of Calabria, where every town, every landscape, and every dish tells a story of a region rich in history and brimming with beauty. Let us uncover the secrets of this enchanting region, from the majestic castles of Roseto Capo Spulico and Cosenza to the archaeological wonders of Locri Epizephyrii and the culinary delights of the Calabrian cuisine.

Welcome to a journey through Calabria, where the allure of the coast is matched only by the charm of its towns and the richness of its cultural heritage. Here, the heart and soul of Southern Italy are waiting to be discovered, offering a travel experience that is as authentic as it is unforgettable. Welcome to the hidden splendor of Calabria, a true Mediterranean paradise waiting to be explored.

Calabria, located in the southernmost part of Italy, is a region overflowing with hidden gems and unexplored treasures. From the stunning coastal towns to the rugged mountain landscapes, this area offers a diverse range of experiences that beautifully showcase its rich history, culture, and natural splendor.

The coastal towns of Calabria are a true highlight, with their crystal-clear turquoise waters, golden sandy beaches, and picturesque fishing villages. Tropea, known as the "Jewel of Calabria," is a breathtaking cliffside town that overlooks the Tyrrhenian Sea. Its narrow streets, historic buildings, and magnificent views are a must-see for any traveler. Not to be missed is Scilla, a charming fishing village where colorful houses cascade down the hillsides, creating a scene straight out of a postcard.

Venturing further into Calabria's diverse landscape, Rocca Imperiale beckons with its imposing castle of Frederick II, perched high on a hill. This medieval fortress, a testament to the region's storied past, offers panoramic views of the surrounding countryside and the Ionian Sea. The town itself, with its labyrinth of streets and rich history, is a captivating discovery.

Nearby, Roseto Capo Spulico, with its own stunning castle, stands as a sentinel over the sea. This fortress, blending Byzantine and Norman architectural styles, overlooks some of the most breathtaking coastal scenery in Calabria, with pristine beaches and azure waters inviting exploration and relaxation.

Beyond the coast, Calabria's landscape transforms into rugged mountains, offering adventure and exploration. The Sila National Park, a nature lover's paradise, features dense forests, pristine lakes, and snow-capped peaks in winter. This park is perfect for hiking, skiing, and wildlife spotting. Nearby, the picturesque village of Morano Calabro, set amidst the mountains, provides an insight into the region's rich history and traditional lifestyle.

In Crotone, the legacy of the ancient philosopher Pythagoras lingers in the air. This city, a significant center of Magna Graecia, boasts not only a rich historical heritage but also stunning natural beauty. Its coastline, with majestic cliffs plunging into the sea, offers some of the most spectacular views in Calabria, complemented by its beautiful beaches and crystal-clear waters.

Calabria's history is also deeply rooted in its numerous archaeological sites and landmarks. The ancient city of Locri Epizephyrii, a Greek foundation, offers well-preserved ruins that take visitors back in time. The Norman Castle of Cosenza, a medieval fortress in the city of Cosenza, stands as a symbol of the region's past struggles and triumphs.

The region is not only rich in natural and historical wonders but also in culinary delights. Calabrian cuisine is a delicious blend of flavors, heavily influenced by its proximity to the sea and agricultural richness. Dishes such as swordfish involtini and the spicy spreadable salami 'nduja highlight the local gastronomy.

The hidden gem of Chianalea di Scilla, reminiscent of Venice with its water-edge homes, offers an enchanting blend of history and romance. The pristine beaches and clear waters of Capo Vaticano are a haven for beach-goers and snorkelers. Stilo, with its Byzantine church, the Cattolica, represents the region's diverse cultural influences.

Le Castella impresses with its Aragonese castle rising from the sea, a testament to Calabria's historical maritime defenses. The abandoned town of Pentedattilo, set against a craggy mountain, offers a unique, otherworldly experience. The ruins of Sibari, an ancient Greek city, invite visitors to uncover the mysteries of Magna Graecia.

In Zungri, the cave settlement provides an intriguing look into ancient living arrangements, while Rossano merges Byzantine history with its unique licorice production. Bivongi contrasts the tranquility of its monastery with the natural splendor of the Marmarico Waterfall. The Sanctuary of San Francesco di Paola embodies Calabria's spiritual heritage.

Calabria's cuisine, characterized by the spicy 'nduja and fresh seafood dishes, reflects the Mediterranean's influence. The region's wine, particularly the Cirò from Cirò Marina, offers a taste of Calabria's rich viticultural history. The people of Calabria, known for their warmth and vibrant traditions, bring life to the region. Traditional festivals, folk dances like the Tarantella, and a welcoming spirit make every visitor feel at home.

In the sun-drenched toe of Italy's boot, Calabria unfurls as a region awash in history, culture, and natural beauty. This less-trodden land of hidden gems, nestled between the azure waters of the Tyrrhenian and Ionian Seas, showcases the quintessence of southern Italy in its rugged landscapes, ancient ruins, and culinary richness.

Embark on a journey through Calabria, where every town, from the stunning cliffs of Tropea to the serene fishing village of Scilla, tells a story steeped in history. Discover the region's many facets, from Rocca Imperiale's historical allure to the Sila National Park's natural splendor.

In Calabria, the culinary experience is as rich and varied as its landscapes. The region's cuisine is a testament to its diverse heritage, with flavors that speak of both the mountains and the sea. Specialties like spicy 'nduja, a spreadable salami with a fiery kick, and tender swordfish involtini reflect Calabria's love for bold flavors and fresh seafood.

The region is also renowned for its cheeses, such as Pecorino del Monte Poro and Caciocavallo Silano DOP, each offering a unique taste of Calabria's pastoral traditions. These cheeses are not just a delight for the palate but also embody the region's deep connection to its land and history.

Calabria's wine culture, deeply ingrained in its identity, offers an exploration of unique flavors. The wines of Calabria, such as the robust Gaglioppo and the refreshing Greco Bianco, are a reflection of the region's varied terroir. They tell a story of a land kissed by the sun and nurtured by the sea, where vineyards stretch across coastal hills and mountain slopes.

In addition to its savory delights, Calabria boasts an array of sweet treats, such as the unique tartufo di Pizzo, a delectable ice cream dessert, and the delicate, honey-laced mostaccioli biscuits. These sweets are not just desserts but a celebration of Calabria's confectionery heritage.

As you wander through the charming streets of Tropea, Scilla, and other Calabrian towns, allow yourself to be seduced by the aromas and flavors of local trattorias and markets. Indulge in dishes that are a fusion of earthy, robust ingredients and the bounty of the sea, each bite a testament to the region's rich culinary culture.

Calabria, a land where the rustic charm of its towns meets the untouched beauty of its coasts and mountains, invites you to indulge in a symphony of flavors. From fiery salami to aromatic wines and creamy cheeses, each element of Calabria's cuisine is a journey into the heart of southern Italy's gastronomic landscape.

Whether savoring a glass of Cirò on a sun-drenched terrace or enjoying a slice of caciocavallo with a view of the rolling hills, Calabria's culinary delights enhance the experience of exploring this enchanting region. It's a place where each meal is an invitation to celebrate the rich tapestry of flavors that make Calabria a hidden Mediterranean paradise.

Beyond its culinary allure, Calabria beckons with diverse experiences, from exploring ancient castles and archaeological wonders to immersing in the natural beauty of its national parks. It's a region that promises not just breathtaking views and historical discoveries but also an intimate encounter with the soul of Italy's deep south.

Often overlooked but unforgettable, Calabria invites travelers to discover its coastal charm, mountainous adventures, rich history, and vibrant culture. Each town, landscape, and dish in Calabria tells its own unique story, awaiting exploration and appreciation.

4.7 Off-the-Beaten-Path in Sicily

In the heart of the Mediterranean Sea lies Sicily, an island of ancient history, diverse landscapes, and rich cultural heritage. As the largest island in the Mediterranean, Sicily is a world unto itself, where the vibrancy of Italian culture meets the legacy of civilizations that have shaped its past. This enchanting island, often overshadowed by the bustling cities of mainland Italy, is a land of hidden gems and unexplored treasures, waiting to be discovered by those who venture off the beaten path.

Sicily is not just a destination; it's a journey through time and nature, where the remnants of ancient empires coexist with the beauty of the present. From the historic streets of Palermo to the stunning landscapes of the Aeolian Islands, and from the archaeological wonders of Siracusa to the baroque splendor of Noto, Sicily invites you to explore its many facets.

Join us on this exploration of Sicily, where every town, every landscape, and every dish tells a story of an island rich in history and brimming with beauty. Let us uncover the secrets of this enchanting island, from the serene beaches of Cefalù to the dramatic cliffs of the Zingaro Nature Reserve, and from the ancient ruins of Agrigento to the vibrant markets of Catania.

Welcome to a journey through Sicily, where the allure of the past meets the charm of the present, offering a travel experience that is as authentic as it is unforgettable. Let us embark on this discovery of Italy's hidden gem, where the heart and soul of the Mediterranean are waiting to be explored. Welcome to the hidden splendor of Sicily, a true Mediterranean paradise waiting to be discovered.

Sicily, the largest island in the Mediterranean Sea, is a land of mesmerizing landscapes, profound history, and distinctive culture. It's a place where the past and present converge in the most beautiful ways. While many tourists gravitate towards well-known destinations like Palermo, Taormina, and Siracusa, the true essence of Sicily can often be found in its hidden corners, where a quieter and more authentic experience awaits.

The town of Cefalù, nestled on the northern coast of the island, is one such hidden gem. With its quaint streets, picturesque harbor, and the stunning backdrop of a Norman cathedral, Cefalù offers a slice of Sicilian life that remains untarnished by the passage of time. Visitors can meander through its labyrinthine alleys, savoring local delicacies, and immerse themselves in the relaxed, almost timeless ambiance. The town's rich tapestry of history is visible in every corner, with ancient ruins and medieval architecture providing a window into the island's multifaceted past.

Venturing further, the Aeolian Islands emerge as a spectacular off-the-beaten-path destination. This volcanic archipelago, sprinkled to the north of the main island, is a world unto itself. Islands like Lipari, Vulcano, and Stromboli beckon with their untouched beaches, hiking trails leading to volcanic craters, and the freshest of seafood. For nature enthusiasts and those seeking solitude, the Aeolian Islands offer a haven of biodiversity and a serene escape from the lively tourist hubs. The sight of Stromboli's active volcano, erupting periodically, is a humbling reminder of nature's might and beauty.

On the northwest coast, the Zingaro Nature Reserve stands as a testament to Sicily's unspoiled natural beauty. This protected area, with its rugged cliffs, crystal-clear waters, and diverse wildlife, is a paradise for nature lovers. Hiking along its coastal trails reveals hidden coves and secluded beaches, offering moments of tranquility and a chance to swim in the turquoise embrace of the Mediterranean.

But Sicily's hidden treasures extend far beyond these gems. Ragusa Ibla, with its baroque architecture and winding streets, tells a story of resilience and beauty. The Scala dei Turchi in Realmonte, a striking white cliff that dramatically meets the azure sea, is a sight to behold. Mozia Island in Marsala, with its ancient ruins and salt marshes, offers a glimpse into a rich, bygone era. The Santa Rosalia Hermitage in Palermo, a sanctuary of peace nestled in the mountains, provides a spiritual retreat.

Archaeological enthusiasts will find the Selinunte Archaeological Park and its impressive Greek ruins captivating, while the Cavagrande del Cassibile Nature Reserve, with its canyons and waterfalls, showcases Sicily's diverse landscapes. The picturesque Tonnara di Scopello, a historic tuna processing plant, and the scenic beauty of the Monti Iblei mountain range are not to be missed. In Trapani and Paceco, the ancient saltpans still operate using traditional methods, offering a unique insight into the island's heritage.

Culturally, Sicily is a treasure trove. The Segesta Archaeological Park features a well-preserved Greek temple and an ancient theater, offering a journey back in time. The elegant Donnafugata Castle in Ragusa, surrounded by lush gardens, and the Mangiapane Cave in Custonaci, with its ancient dwellings, are just a few examples of Sicily's rich cultural fabric.

For nature enthusiasts, the Madonie Regional Natural Park, with its diverse flora and fauna, and the Nebrodi Regional Park, a vast expanse of wilderness, are ideal for exploration. The lesser-known access points to Mount Etna, Europe's largest active volcano, offer adventurous paths less traveled. The medieval village of Savoca, immortalized in "The Godfather" movie, and the Vendicari Nature Reserve in Noto, with its sandy beaches and lagoons, are yet other hidden wonders.

Sicily's culinary and viticultural delights are as varied as its landscapes. From the bustling beach town of Mondello, known for its vibrant atmosphere and crystal-clear waters, to the serene fishing village of Sferracavallo, famous for its seafood, Sicily's gastronomic offerings are a feast for the senses.

Sicily's culinary journey is as rich and varied as its landscapes and history. Nestled within this narrative of exploration and discovery are the island's gastronomic treasures, each offering a unique taste of Sicilian heritage.

Discover the world-renowned wines of Sicily, where the sun-drenched vineyards produce exceptional vintages. The island's volcanic soils and unique microclimates give birth to exquisite wines such as the robust Nero d'Avola, the elegant Etna Rosso, and the sweet, amber-hued Marsala. Each glass of Sicilian wine is a reflection of the island's diverse terroir and winemaking tradition, a story of flavor and passion passed down through generations.

Sicilian cuisine, a tapestry of Mediterranean influences, is a feast for the senses. Experience the island's culinary diversity with dishes like Caponata, a sweet and sour eggplant dish, and the iconic Arancini, crispy rice balls filled with savory delights. Sicily's coastal towns offer a bounty of fresh seafood, while the inland regions bring forth hearty dishes like Pasta alla Norma, rich with the flavors of tomatoes and eggplant.

Cheese lovers will delight in Sicily's array of artisanal cheeses. Pecorino Siciliano, with its sharp and salty profile, is a testament to the island's pastoral traditions. The creamy Ricotta, a staple in Sicilian desserts such as Cannoli, embodies the island's love for rich, indulgent flavors.

As you journey through Sicily, let these culinary experiences enrich your exploration. From the bustling markets of Palermo to the quaint trattorias nestled in hilltop towns, each meal is an invitation to savor the island's rich gastronomic heritage.

The charm of Sicily lies not only in its celebrated destinations but also in its lesser-known locales like the medieval village of Caccamo, the tranquil Isola delle Femmine, the picturesque Sambuca di Sicilia, and the unique art installation at the Cretto di Burri in Gibellina Vecchia. Each place, each town, each beach, and each mountain tells a story, contributing to the rich tapestry that is Sicily.

This majestic island, with its hidden paradises, invites travelers to venture beyond the familiar and immerse themselves in the authentic, enchanting, and often unexpected experiences it offers. Sicily, with its myriad of hidden gems, beckons the curious and the adventurous to explore its depths and uncover the secrets of southern Italy's most captivating island.

4.8 Delights of the Southern Italian Islands

In the azure waters of the Mediterranean Sea, Southern Italy's islands stand as enchanting oases, each offering a unique blend of natural beauty, rich history, and vibrant culture. From the iconic cliffs of Capri to the volcanic majesty of the Aeolian Islands, and from the serene beauty of Procida to the rugged landscapes of Pantelleria, these islands are a mosaic of diverse experiences, each beckoning travelers to explore their hidden treasures.

These islands are not just destinations; they are stories waiting to be told, landscapes waiting to be explored, and cultures waiting to be experienced. The Southern Italian islands invite you on a journey through crystal-clear waters, ancient ruins, charming villages, and breathtaking natural wonders.

Join us on this exploration of Southern Italy's islands, where every cove, every hilltop, and every street tells a story of a land steeped in history and brimming with beauty. Let us uncover the secrets of these enchanting islands, from the tranquil beaches of the Tremiti Islands to the cultural richness of the Egadi Islands, and from the unspoiled nature of the Pontine Islands to the vibrant traditions of the Sardinian archipelago.

Welcome to a journey through Southern Italy's islands, where the allure of the sea meets the charm of the land, offering a travel experience that is as authentic as it is unforgettable. Let us embark on this discovery of Italy's hidden gems, where the heart and soul of the Mediterranean are waiting to be explored. Welcome to the hidden splendor of Southern Italy's islands, a true Mediterranean paradise waiting to be discovered.

One of the most enchanting islands in Southern Italy is Procida, located in the Bay of Naples. A kaleidoscope of pastel-colored houses, narrow, winding streets, and a picturesque harbor that seems to have leapt straight out of a vibrant painting, Procida is a treasure trove of tranquility and charm. Visitors can leisurely explore the island by foot, soaking in its authentic atmosphere, and admiring the breathtaking views of the Mediterranean Sea. Each corner of Procida tells a story, a whisper from the past, making it a living canvas of Italian culture and history.

Venturing further, the island of Pantelleria, situated between Sicily and Tunisia, emerges as a stark contrast with its volcanic landscapes and rejuvenating thermal springs. This unique island offers a wellness experience unlike any other. Travelers seeking serenity can indulge in therapeutic mud baths, relax in soothing natural hot springs, and take in the captivating beauty of the island's rugged coastline. Pantelleria, with its dramatic cliffs and panoramic sea views, is a haven for those looking to escape the ordinary.

The island of Lampedusa, floating in the Mediterranean Sea, is a cultural jewel. A vibrant blend of Italian and African influences, Lampedusa is a melting pot of traditions and histories. Visitors can embark on a cultural journey through the island's ancient ruins, stroll through the quaint fishing village of Rabbit Beach, and be mesmerized by the incredible marine life in the protected waters surrounding the island. Lampedusa is not just an island; it's a crossroads of civilizations, each leaving its indelible mark.

In the Aeolian Islands, a volcanic archipelago off the coast of Sicily, adventure and tranquility coexist in harmony. Each island in the Aeolian archipelago has its own distinct personality. From the fiery eruptions of Stromboli, offering a spectacular natural fireworks display, to the serene and verdant landscapes of Salina, these islands are a mosaic of natural wonders. Whether it's hiking to the smoking summit of Stromboli, exploring the verdant pathways of Salina, or lounging on the sun-kissed beaches of Lipari, the Aeolian Islands are a testament to nature's artistry.

Further to the region of Lazio, the islands of Ponza, Ventotene, Palmarola, Zannone, and Gavi are hidden gems waiting to be uncovered. These islands are a symphony of natural beauty, historical allure, and cultural richness. From their sun-drenched beaches and crystal-clear waters to the quaint charm of their towns, each island offers a unique escape into a world of relaxation and exploration. These islands are not just destinations; they are portals to an ancient, yet ever-vibrant way of life.

Heading south to the heart of Puglia, the Tremiti Islands emerge as a constellation of beauty in the Adriatic Sea. This archipelago, made up of San Domino, San Nicola, Capraia, Cretaccio, and Pianosa, is a tapestry woven with stories of pirates, saints, and natural wonders. Each island presents its own unique charm, from San Domino's lush forests to San Nicola's historical allure, offering a journey through time and nature. The Tremiti Islands are a blend of myth and reality, where legends seem to come alive against the backdrop of stunning landscapes.

In the vibrant region of Campania, the islands of Capri, Ischia, Procida, Vivara, and Nisida await with open arms. Capri is a jewel of glamour and natural splendor, with its iconic Faraglioni rocks and the enchanting Blue Grotto. Ischia, a haven of wellness, is famed for its thermal springs and luxurious spas. Vivara and Nisida, lesser-known but equally captivating, are sanctuaries for wildlife and nature enthusiasts. These islands are not just places; they are experiences, each offering a unique glimpse into the soul of Southern Italy.

Sicily, the crown jewel of the Mediterranean, is surrounded by an array of magical islands. The Aeolian Islands, with their volcanic peaks and azure waters, are a paradise for explorers and beach lovers alike. The Egadi Islands, a haven for snorkelers and divers, reveal an underwater world of wonder. Pantelleria, Lampedusa, Linosa, and Ustica each shine with their own distinctive charm, offering a mosaic of experiences from rugged landscapes to serene beaches.

Finally, the majestic island of Sardinia, with its rugged coastlines and emerald waters, is a land of timeless beauty. The La Maddalena Archipelago, with islands like La Maddalena, Caprera, Spargi, Santo Stefano, Santa Maria, Budelli, and Razzoli, is a haven for those who seek communion with pristine nature. And the islands of San Pietro and Sant'Antioco, with their unique landscapes and rich histories, are hidden treasures in the Mediterranean mosaic.

In the heart of the Mediterranean, the Southern Italian islands are not only a feast for the eyes but also a paradise for the palate. Each island boasts its own unique culinary traditions, offering an array of gastronomic experiences that are as diverse and rich as their landscapes and histories.

On the sun-kissed island of Capri, the vineyards produce exquisite wines that capture the essence of the island's terroir. Capri Bianco, a crisp and refreshing white, and Capri Rosso, a full-bodied red, are perfect accompaniments to the island's seafood-centric cuisine. Caprese salad, made with fresh local tomatoes, mozzarella, and basil, is a simple yet iconic dish that embodies the flavors of Capri.

The volcanic soil of the Aeolian Islands, particularly on Salina, gives rise to the renowned Malvasia delle Lipari, a sweet wine with a complex bouquet. This nectar pairs beautifully with the island's rich cuisine, including dishes like "Pasta al forno con melanzane," a hearty baked pasta with eggplants.

Procida, with its colorful harbors and fertile soil, is known for its delightful "Lingue di Procida," a lemon-flavored cake that's a testament to the island's abundant citrus groves. The island's cuisine also features fresh seafood, with "Spaghetti ai frutti di mare" being a local favorite.

In Pantelleria, the unique Passito di Pantelleria wine, made from Zibibbo grapes, is a sweet indulgence, perfect as a dessert wine or as an accompaniment to the island's savory dishes. The island's capers, another local gem, add a burst of flavor to dishes like "Pasta con capperi e pomodori."

The Tremiti Islands, with their crystal-clear waters, offer a bounty of fresh seafood, reflected in dishes like "Zuppa di pesce," a rich and flavorful fish soup. The local olive oil, made from olives grown in the island's groves, enhances every dish with its fruity notes.

Sardinia, a land of robust flavors and ancient culinary traditions, is renowned for its Pecorino Sardo, a sheep's milk cheese with a rich and tangy flavor. The island's wines, including the robust Cannonau and the crisp Vermentino, are perfect pairings for Sardinian specialties like "Porceddu," a spit-roasted suckling pig, and "Culurgiones," a type of stuffed pasta.

Sicily, the jewel of the Mediterranean, offers a culinary journey through its diverse landscape. From the sweet Marsala wine to the island's signature dish, "Arancini," rice balls filled with ragù, peas, and mozzarella, Sicily's cuisine is a celebration of flavors. The island's cheeses, such as the piquant Caciocavallo and creamy Ricotta, add depth to its rich culinary tapestry.

Each island's culinary offerings are a reflection of its history, landscape, and culture. From the terraced vineyards of Capri to the aromatic kitchens of

Sicily, the Southern Italian islands invite you to indulge in a symphony of tastes that are as enchanting as their sun-drenched shores and ancient ruins.

In conclusion, whether you're seeking a tranquil beach retreat, a journey through culture and history, or an adventure in the great outdoors, the Southern Italian islands offer an escapade that will captivate your heart and leave you yearning for more. These islands, with their pristine beauty, rich heritage, and unique cultural tapestry, are not just destinations; they are invitations to experience the very essence of Italy.

Chapter 5: Hidden Gems of Italy's Islands

5.1 Hidden Gems of the Tuscan Archipelago

In the embrace of the Tyrrhenian Sea, off the serene Tuscan coast, lies an enchanting constellation of islands known as the Tuscan Archipelago. This collection of islands, seven main and several smaller ones, is a tapestry of uncharted beauty and historical mystique, beckoning those who seek to venture beyond the usual tourist trails. As we embark on a journey through this archipelago, each island unfolds as a chapter of a captivating narrative, offering a blend of pristine natural splendors, rich cultural heritage, and tranquil escapes.

The Tuscan Archipelago is not just a destination; it is a journey into the heart of Italy's maritime soul, where the rhythm of the waves dictates the pace of life and where every cove, cliff, and village tells a story steeped in time. From the tranquil shores of Giglio Island to the historical richness of Elba, the rugged allure of Capraia, and the undiscovered corners of Pianosa, Montecristo, Giannutri, and Gorgona, this archipelago offers a mosaic of experiences that beckon the explorer within.

As we sail through these hidden gems, we discover not only the untouched beauty of the islands but also the essence of a quieter, more authentic Italy. The Tuscan Archipelago invites us to leave behind the crowded tourist spots and step into a world where nature's beauty is in its rawest form, where history whispers from ancient ruins, and where the spirit of adventure is rekindled. Let us set sail on this voyage of discovery, where each island awaits with its unique charm, ready to reveal its secrets to those who dare to explore.

EXPLORING ITALY'S HIDDEN GEMS

The Tuscan Archipelago, situated off the coast of Tuscany in Italy, presents a plethora of hidden treasures waiting to be discovered. Comprising seven main islands and several smaller ones, this archipelago offers a unique and enchanting experience for travelers seeking to escape crowded tourist hotspots.

Among these hidden gems, Giglio Island stands out as a true paradise for nature enthusiasts and those in search of a tranquil retreat. With its pristine beaches, crystal-clear waters, and picturesque villages, Giglio exudes a serene ambiance that is perfect for relaxation. Visitors can immerse themselves in the island's natural beauty, taking leisurely walks along the shore or simply basking in the sun while enjoying the gentle sound of the waves.

Another gem within the Tuscan Archipelago is Elba, the third-largest island in Italy. Renowned for its stunning landscapes, which encompass rugged coastlines, lush forests, and vibrant Mediterranean flora, Elba provides a plethora of outdoor activities for adventure enthusiasts. Hiking along the island's scenic trails, snorkeling in its azure waters, or sailing across its captivating coastline are just a few examples of the adventures that await visitors on Elba. Additionally, the island boasts a rich historical heritage, with remnants of ancient civilizations and the famous exile of Napoleon Bonaparte.

For those seeking a truly off-the-beaten-path experience, Capraia Island is an ideal choice. With its rugged terrain and untouched nature, Capraia offers a haven for hikers and adventure seekers. The island's secluded coves and hidden caves provide excellent opportunities for snorkeling and diving, revealing a mesmerizing world of underwater wonders waiting to be discovered.

But the Tuscan Archipelago doesn't end there. It also includes other hidden gems such as Pianosa, Montecristo, Giannutri, and Gorgona, each offering its own unique charm and beauty. Pianosa, with its unspoiled beaches and tranquil atmosphere, provides a peaceful escape from the hustle and bustle of daily life. Montecristo, known for its wild and untouched nature, offers a sense of isolation and serenity that is hard to find elsewhere. Giannutri, with its beautiful cliffs and crystal-clear waters, is a paradise for snorkelers and divers. Gorgona, the smallest island in the archipelago, is a nature lover's dream, home to a rich variety of wildlife and captivating landscapes.

Exploring the hidden gems of the Tuscan Archipelago allows travelers to discover Italy's lesser-known treasures and create memories that will last a lifetime. From the unspoiled beaches to the diverse wildlife and captivating history, each island holds the key to an unforgettable experience. Whether it's relaxing on the shores of Giglio, embarking on an outdoor adventure on Elba, or immersing yourself in the untamed beauty of Capraia, the Tuscan Archipelago offers something truly special for every traveler.

5.2 Exploring the Authenticity of the Pontine Islands

Off the beaten path of Italy's celebrated landscapes, in the heart of the Tyrrhenian Sea, lies a cluster of islands untouched by the passage of time and the rush of the modern world. The Pontine Islands, a hidden archipelago off the central coast, beckon those with a spirit of adventure and a yearning for discovery. Comprising six main islands - Ponza, Ventotene, Palmarola, Zannone, Gavi, and Santo Stefano - each with its unique allure, these islands are a mosaic of natural wonders, historical mysteries, and the enduring charm of Italian culture.

As we set sail on this journey of exploration, we venture into a realm where the azure of the sea meets the lush greenery of unspoiled landscapes, where ancient history whispers in the breeze, and where every cove and cliff tells a story. From Ponza's underwater paradises to Ventotene's Roman relics, the rugged beauty of Palmarola, the biodiversity of Zannone, the secluded shores of Gavi, and the historical echoes of Santo Stefano, the Pontine Islands are a canvas of experiences waiting to be painted by the discerning traveler.

This journey through the Pontine Islands is not just a trip across the sea; it's an odyssey through time and nature, an invitation to step off the well-trodden path and immerse oneself in the authentic heart of Italy. Let us embark on this voyage to discover the hidden gems of the Tyrrhenian Sea, where each island offers a unique story, a different adventure, and an unforgettable slice of Italian paradise.

Nestled off the coast of central Italy, the Pontine Islands await intrepid travelers seeking a unique and authentic escape. This captivating archipelago comprises six main islands: Ponza, Ventotene, Palmarola, Zannone, Gavi, and Santo Stefano. Each island offers a distinct character and a trove of experiences waiting to be explored.

Ponza: A Snorkeler's Paradise. Ponza, the largest of the group, is celebrated for its dramatic cliffs, secluded coves, and vibrant marine life. Crystal-clear waters beckon snorkeling and diving enthusiasts to uncover the hidden treasures beneath the surface. Colorful fish, thriving coral reefs, and mesmerizing underwater caves make this island a paradise for underwater exploration. On the surface, you'll find charming villages, lively markets, and seaside restaurants where you can savor freshly caught seafood.

Ventotene: A Journey Through Roman History. Ventotene, an island with a rich Roman history, invites history buffs to wander through its well-preserved archaeological sites. The grand Villa Giulia and the ancient Roman Port provide a fascinating glimpse into the island's storied past. Beyond its historical allure, Ventotene boasts a charming village with narrow streets, local shops, and welcoming trattorias. It's a place where the echoes of ancient civilizations blend seamlessly with modern life.

Palmarola: Nature's Wonderland. Palmarola, designated as a nature reserve, is a paradise for nature lovers. Rugged landscapes, lush greenery, and diverse wildlife make it a haven for hikers and birdwatchers. Explore scenic hiking trails that offer breathtaking vistas of the surrounding sea and other islands. As the sun sets, the island's tranquility and untouched beauty create a sense of wonder and serenity.

Zannone: A Sanctuary of Biodiversity. Zannone, a sanctuary for rare flora and fauna, is a hidden gem for those seeking an untouched natural environment. Explore its pristine beaches, hike through its wild interior, and witness the rich biodiversity that calls this island home. Birdwatchers will be delighted by the variety of avian species that inhabit the island, adding to its allure as a natural paradise.

Gavi: Secluded Beach Bliss. Gavi's secluded beaches and crystal-clear waters offer a serene escape from the everyday hustle and bustle. The island's untouched beauty and peaceful atmosphere make it an ideal destination for relaxation and tranquility. Bask in the sun, swim in the clear waters, or take leisurely walks along the pristine shores.

Santo Stefano: History and Natural Beauty Combined. Santo Stefano, once a prison island, now seamlessly blends historical ruins with natural beauty. Explore the remnants of its past, including the old penitentiary and watchtowers. Hike through its rugged terrain, where dramatic cliffs meet the sea, creating postcard-worthy views. Santo Stefano's unique blend of history and natural wonders offers a truly unforgettable experience.

The Pontine Islands, with their serene environment and authentic local culture, provide an ideal retreat from bustling tourist crowds. Savor traditional cuisine in a relaxed setting, where fresh seafood and locally sourced ingredients take center stage.

For the adventurous traveler, the Pontine Islands offer a hidden gem ripe for exploration. Whether you're drawn to Ponza's lively charm, Ventotene's historical allure, or Zannone's pristine tranquility, each island caters to diverse preferences. The Pontine Islands embody the essence of off-the-beaten-path exploration, inviting you to uncover Italy's often-overlooked natural and historical wonders.

In summary, the Pontine Islands offer not only picturesque beaches and scenic hiking trails but also a captivating window into ancient Roman history. This harmonious blend of natural beauty, cultural depth, and adventure ensures a memorable and truly authentic Italian experience. Explore, discover, and create memories that will last a lifetime in this hidden gem of the Tyrrhenian Sea.

5.3 Off-the-Beaten-Path in the Maddalena Archipelago

In the shimmering Tyrrhenian Sea, off the northeastern coast of Sardinia, lies an archipelago of unparalleled beauty, a cluster of islands where nature's artistry and history's whispers converge. The Maddalena Archipelago, a hidden gem in the crown of Italy's maritime treasures, beckons those in search of serene landscapes, translucent waters, and tales as old as time. Comprising seven main islands and numerous islets, each island in the archipelago offers a unique adventure, a chance to step into a world where the rhythms of island life dictate the day.

Here, amidst this cluster of islands, the dance of the sea and land has sculpted scenes of breathtaking beauty, from the vibrant town of La Maddalena to the historical echoes of Caprera, the untouched wilderness of Budelli, Razzoli's rugged allure, Santa Maria's tranquil shores, the pristine Spargi, and the elusive Santo Stefano. These islands are not just spots on the map but realms of exploration and discovery, where every cove tells a story, every beach holds a secret, and every trail leads to wonders yet unseen.

As we journey through the Maddalena Archipelago, we are not just traversing the waters of the Tyrrhenian Sea; we are navigating through a rich tapestry of history, culture, and natural splendor. This is a voyage into the heart of the Mediterranean, a journey that invites you to bask in the sun on white sandy beaches, delve into the depths of history, and surrender to the allure of Italy's most enchanting islands. Welcome to the Maddalena Archipelago, where every island is a chapter in a story of timeless beauty and enduring charm.

When it comes to exploring Italy's hidden gems, one cannot overlook the enchanting Maddalena Archipelago, nestled in the crystal-clear waters of the Tyrrhenian Sea. Comprising seven main islands and numerous smaller islets, the Maddalena Archipelago is a paradise waiting to be discovered.

La Maddalena Island (Isola Maddalena). Situated at the heart of the archipelago, La Maddalena Island is the main inhabited island and offers a range of tourist services. Its white sandy beaches and crystal-clear waters are perfect for swimming and snorkeling. The town of La Maddalena itself, with its colorful houses and bustling streets, exudes a charming atmosphere. Strolling through the narrow alleyways, you'll find quaint shops selling local crafts and delicious gelato.

Caprera Island (Isola Caprera). This island is famous for being the home of Giuseppe Garibaldi, one of the founding fathers of modern Italy. Today, his museum, which includes Garibaldi's residence and mausoleum, is open to visitors. Caprera is also known for its wild beaches and picturesque coves.

Budelli Island (Isola Budelli). Budelli's main attraction is Spiaggia Rosa, a unique pink sand beach, thanks to its pink coral grains. Access to this beach may be regulated to preserve its integrity, but the island offers other stunning coves and beaches to explore.

Razzoli Island (Isola Razzoli): This island boasts wild landscapes with rugged cliffs and spectacular panoramic views. It's perfect for hiking, offering plenty of opportunities for nature lovers and photographers.

Santa Maria Island (Isola Santa Maria). Ideal for swimming and sunbathing enthusiasts, this island features white sandy beaches and turquoise waters, creating an idyllic setting for relaxation and leisure by the sea.

Spargi Island (Isola Spargi). As an uninhabited island, Spargi offers pristine beaches and tranquil coves. Nature enthusiasts will appreciate the untouched beauty of the island. Explore hidden coves and secret swimming spots on a boat tour around the island, and don't miss the opportunity for snorkeling in the crystal-clear waters to marvel at the vibrant underwater world.

Santo Stefano Island (Isola Santo Stefano). Situated within the Maddalena Archipelago, Santo Stefano Island is privately owned, with some areas occupied by the Italian Navy. Despite its private status, the island's breathtaking natural beauty can be admired from the surrounding coastline, often included in boat excursions of the archipelago.

In conclusion, the Maddalena Archipelago offers a truly off-the-beaten-path experience for those seeking to explore Italy's hidden gems. From the charming town of La Maddalena to the untouched islands of Caprera, Budelli, Razzoli, Santa Maria, Spargi, and the unique Santo Stefano Island, this archipelago is a treasure trove of natural beauty, cultural heritage, and opportunities for relaxation and adventure. Whether you're a history buff, an outdoor enthusiast, or simply in search of tranquility, the Maddalena Archipelago has something to offer everyone.

5.4 Delights of the Tremiti Islands

In the heart of the Adriatic Sea, where the waters dance with the light of the sun, lies a cluster of islands that remain one of Italy's best-kept secrets. The Tremiti Islands, set off the coast of Puglia, emerge as a mosaic of natural beauty and historical intrigue, waiting to be explored by those who venture beyond the familiar. This archipelago, with its five distinct islands - San Domino, San Nicola, Capraia, Cretaccio, and Pianosa - invites travelers to step into a world where the hustle of the mainland fades into the tranquil rhythms of island life.

Here, in this secluded paradise, the islands weave a tapestry of experiences that blend the azure of the sea with the green of the Mediterranean landscape. Each island, with its unique character, offers a doorway to adventures and serenity alike, beckoning visitors to discover their hidden coves, ancient ruins, and vibrant marine life. From the historical richness of San Nicola to the lush natural beauty of San Domino, and the untouched wilderness of Capraia, Cretaccio, and Pianosa, the Tremiti Islands are a canvas of experiences waiting to be painted by the curious and the adventurous.

As we embark on this journey through the Tremiti Islands, we are not just traveling to a destination; we are journeying through time, nature, and culture. We are invited to dive into the crystal-clear waters, to wander along cobblestone streets steeped in history, and to bask in the serenity of Italy's hidden maritime jewels. Let this be an exploration of not just the beauty of the islands but also of the spirit they encapsulate – a spirit of discovery, of tranquility, and of the enduring charm of the Adriatic Sea.

Nestled in the Adriatic Sea off the coast of Puglia, the Tremiti Islands are a hidden gem ripe for exploration. This archipelago, comprising San Domino, San Nicola, Capraia, Cretaccio, and Pianosa, offers a delightful respite from the bustling mainland. These islands enchant visitors with their crystal-clear turquoise waters, picturesque beaches, and rugged cliffs, forming a haven for nature lovers and beach aficionados. They present an array of activities for those seeking either a peaceful retreat or an adventurous escape.

San Nicola is the administrative hub of the archipelago and a treasure trove of history and culture. The island's cobblestone streets lead to charming corners of the historic center, perfect for leisurely strolls. One of the highlights is the Abbey of Santa Maria a Mare, a medieval fortress that offers panoramic views of the archipelago. San Nicola's rocky coastline provides excellent opportunities for snorkeling and diving, allowing you to immerse yourself in the mesmerizing underwater world.

As the largest and most inhabited island of the Tremiti, San Domino boasts a range of tourist facilities, restaurants, and cafes. Its sandy beach, Cala delle Arene, is a perfect spot for sunbathing and swimming in the turquoise waters. San Domino is surrounded by lush Mediterranean vegetation, with scenic trails ideal for hiking and biking.

For those seeking a tranquil and natural escape, Capraia is the perfect choice. Although uninhabited, its rocky coasts and crystalline waters make it ideal for kayaking, swimming, and snorkeling. The island's hiking trails offer stunning vistas and opportunities for exploration.

This large clayey rock formation, located close to San Domino and San Nicola, provides a unique perspective on the archipelago's geology. Boat excursions often include a visit to this fascinating geological wonder.

A rocky plateau, also uninhabited, Pianosa is a natural oasis where flora and fauna flourish undisturbed. Exploring its hiking trails allows you to witness the island's untouched beauty, including its rugged rocky beaches.

The Tremiti Islands offer a plethora of opportunities for snorkeling and diving in vibrant marine habitats, allowing you to immerse yourself in the mesmerizing underwater world. With colorful coral reefs and an abundance of marine life, these waters provide an unforgettable experience for snorkelers and divers alike. For those who prefer to stay above the surface, hiking trails await, leading explorers to hidden caves nestled amidst the lush greenery. The islands also boast ancient ruins that offer a glimpse into the past, inviting history enthusiasts to step back in time.

A key attraction on San Domino is the renowned Cala delle Arene beach, boasting a unique rocky arch formation that adds to its natural charm. This picturesque beach is perfect for unwinding and swimming in the azure waters. For a more adventurous experience, visitors can embark on kayak or boat expeditions to explore the Grotta delle Viole and other sea caves. These mystical underground realms are adorned with mesmerizing stalactites and stalagmites, captivating the imagination of all who venture inside.

Rich in history, the Tremiti Islands bear traces of ancient civilizations dating back to the Roman era. On San Nicola, the impressive Abbey of Santa Maria a Mare stands as a medieval fortress, offering panoramic views of the archipelago. The islands' intriguing past as a prison during the Fascist regime adds a poignant layer to their story, with remnants of prison cells still visible today. Exploring the islands allows visitors to not only appreciate their natural beauty but also uncover the fascinating tales of their historical significance.

Culinary experiences on the Tremiti Islands are a highlight, featuring an abundance of fresh seafood and traditional Adriatic flavors. Dining at waterfront restaurants allows visitors to savor the catch of the day, from succulent freshly caught fish to exquisite seafood pasta dishes. For a more casual dining experience, enjoying a beachside picnic provides an opportunity to indulge in local delicacies while surrounded by the captivating beauty of the islands. Whether you're seeking relaxation, adventure, or a taste of history, the Tremiti Islands offer a truly enchanting escape in the Adriatic.

5.5 Lesser-Known Wonders of the Egadi Islands

As the Mediterranean Sea whispers tales of ancient civilizations and hidden paradises, there lies a cluster of islands where time seems to stand still, and nature's beauty remains untamed by the modern world. The Egadi Islands, a trio of secluded jewels off the western coast of Sicily, beckon with the allure of a secret yet to be unveiled. These islands, rich in history and bursting with natural splendor, offer an escape not just from the physical confines of everyday life, but also an invitation to a world where every cove and cliff tells a story, and every wave sings a song of the deep blue sea.

Nestled in these waters, Favignana, Levanzo, and Marettimo emerge as guardians of a bygone era, each holding its own key to a treasure chest of experiences. From Favignana's historical echoes of the tuna trade to Levanzo's prehistoric whispers and Marettimo's rugged, untamed beauty, these islands weave a tapestry of tales as deep and vast as the sea itself.

Here, where the crystal-clear turquoise waters meet the dramatic rocky cliffs and picturesque beaches, the Egadi Islands are not just a destination but a journey back in time, a voyage across the waves of history, and an exploration into the heart of nature's most pristine creations. Let us embark on this journey to discover the hidden wonders of the Egadi Islands, a serene haven where the past and present merge beneath the Sicilian sun.

Located off the western coast of Sicily, the Egadi Islands—Favignana, Levanzo, and Marettimo—are a well-kept secret waiting to be discovered. These islands are a captivating escape, offering unspoiled natural beauty often overlooked by tourists. With crystal-clear turquoise waters, dramatic rocky cliffs, and picturesque beaches, the Egadi Islands provide a serene getaway away from the hustle and bustle of more popular destinations. Whether you're a nature enthusiast, a history buff, or simply seeking tranquility, these islands offer a diverse range of experiences.

Favignana, the largest island, is steeped in maritime history, evident in its ancient Tonnara tuna fishery. Its beaches, like Cala Rossa and Cala Azzurra, are renowned for their stunning azure waters and rocky landscapes. The town center, with its quaint shops and seafood restaurants, offers a glimpse into the island's vibrant culture.

Levanzo, the smallest of the trio, is a haven of peace and prehistoric art. The Grotta del Genovese, with its Neolithic paintings, offers a fascinating peek into ancient human history. Its tranquil streets are lined with whitewashed houses, offering serene sea views and a quiet escape from the modern world.

Marettimo, rugged and mountainous, is perfect for those who love hiking and exploring nature. It boasts a charming village with rustic fishermen's houses and friendly locals, adding to its authentic island charm. Marettimo's pathways lead to panoramic vistas and ancient Roman ruins, making it a treasure trove for adventurers.

One of the highlights of a visit to the Egadi Islands is the Aegadian Marine Protected Area, teeming with marine life. Here, snorkeling and diving enthusiasts will find an underwater paradise, with vibrant coral reefs, schools of fish, and hidden sea caves.

The islands' cuisine is another highlight, with an array of seafood dishes that reflect Sicilian culinary traditions. Beyond the famous couscous di pesce, a seafood stew, the islands offer a variety of dishes featuring fresh tuna, caponata, and pasta with sea urchins. Local wines and almond-based desserts complement these gastronomic delights.

For those seeking an off-the-beaten-path destination in Italy, the Egadi Islands are a perfect choice. Their untouched beauty, rich history, and warm hospitality make them a captivating destination for relaxation, adventure, or cultural immersion. An experience in the Egadi Islands beckons a return visit, promising memories that will last a lifetime. So, pack your bags and embark on an adventure of discovery in this hidden gem of the Mediterranean.

5.6 Secrets of the Aeolian Islands

Sailing across the azure waters of the Tyrrhenian Sea, where the whispers of ancient myths blend seamlessly with the lull of the waves, lies a realm suspended between the sky and the sea. The Aeolian Islands, a constellation of seven gems, rise majestically off the northeastern coast of Sicily, each island an ode to the diverse tapestry of nature's grandeur. Shrouded in legend and rich with history, these islands are a siren call to those who seek to unravel the mysteries of a land sculpted by fire, wind, and wave.

In this celestial dance of land and sea, each island of this archipelago holds its own secrets, waiting to be unveiled. The Aeolian Islands are not mere geographical entities; they are living, breathing canvases of nature's artistry, steeped in the lore of gods and giants, and echoing with the footsteps of ancient civilizations. They beckon the modern explorer to embark on a journey that transcends the bounds of ordinary travel, inviting them to witness the harmonious coexistence of unspoiled nature and rich cultural heritage.

As we embark on this journey through the Aeolian Islands, we are not merely visitors but participants in an ongoing narrative that spans millennia. We are invited to tread lightly on these sacred shores, to listen to the stories whispered by the winds, and to gaze upon landscapes that have captivated the hearts of travelers since time immemorial.

Let us set sail on this voyage of discovery, where the Aeolian Islands emerge as characters in their own right, each island a distinct voice in a chorus of natural splendor and historical resonance. From the vibrant shores of Lipari to the serene landscapes of Salina, the primordial force of Vulcano, the fiery spectacle of Stromboli, the elegant serenity of Panarea, the untouched beauty of Filicudi, and the tranquil seclusion of Alicudi, this is a journey into the very soul of the Mediterranean. Welcome to the Aeolian Islands, where every horizon tells a story and every sunset sings a ballad of the ancient sea.

The Aeolian Islands, nestled off the northeastern coast of Sicily, beckon adventurous travelers to embark on a journey of discovery amidst their enchanting hidden wonders. This captivating archipelago, consisting of seven diverse islands, each possesses a unique allure that is waiting to be explored and experienced.

Lipari, the pulsating heart of this mystical archipelago, offers a vibrant tapestry of history, culture, and stunning natural beauty. The ancient walls of the Lipari Castle stand as silent sentinels of history, while the powdery beaches such as Canneto and Spiaggia Bianca whisper tales of the azure Mediterranean.

Salina, draped in emerald robes of lush vegetation, sings a siren song of tranquil beauty. Its sweet Malvasia wine, like nectar, captures the essence of the island's sun-kissed slopes, while the quaint village of Pollara, immortalized in 'Il Postino', offers a picturesque haven of serenity.

Vulcano, the island born of fire, bewitches with its therapeutic mud baths and simmering fumaroles. Its black sand beaches and the majestic Gran Cratere stand as testaments to the island's fiery origins, inviting the brave to witness nature's raw power.

Stromboli, the untamed and fiery spirit of the archipelago, performs its nightly pyrotechnic dance, casting a mesmerizing glow over the sea. The island's rugged beauty, etched against the night sky, is a spectacle of nature's unfettered might.

Panarea, the smallest jewel in this Aeolian crown, radiates an aura of understated elegance and chic charm. Its secluded coves and prehistoric ruins are a mosaic of timeless beauty, while the island's effervescent nightlife sparkles under the Mediterranean stars.

Filicudi, a bastion of untouched splendor, beckons the soul to embrace its tranquil shores and rugged paths. Here, time meanders lazily, and the panoramic vistas offer a silent ode to the island's pristine and enduring beauty.

Alicudi, the most remote whisper of land in this archipelago, offers a refuge of unparalleled peace. A world apart, it invites a communion with a simpler, more elemental way of life, amidst dramatic cliffs and terraced gardens that cascade down to the cobalt sea.

The Aeolian Islands, each a unique chapter in an epic tale, extend an invitation to those who seek not just a destination, but an experience etched in the heart and soul. From Lipari's pulsating allure to Salina's vine-kissed hills, Vulcano's earthy power, Stromboli's fiery heart, Panarea's elegant whispers, Filicudi's silent beauty, and Alicudi's timeless embrace, these islands promise an odyssey of wonder, a journey of discovery that resonates long after the journey has ended.

5.7 Hidden Cultural Gems of the Pelagie Islands

Embarking on a voyage to the southernmost frontier of the Italian seas, where the Mediterranean unfurls its azure canvas, lies a cluster of islands woven from the threads of myth and reality. The Pelagie Islands, floating like emerald and sapphire jewels in the sun-kissed waters, invite the discerning traveler to a realm where time holds a different meaning, and nature's artwork is displayed in its most pristine form. This is a world where the whispers of history, the rhythm of traditional life, and the unblemished beauty of nature coalesce to create a tapestry of experiences both profound and enchanting.

Here, in this secluded corner of the world, each island - Lampedusa, Linosa, and Lampione - tells its own story, a narrative steeped in the rich tapestry of Mediterranean culture, flavored by the salt of the sea and the warmth of the sun. From the multicultural vibrancy of Lampedusa to the volcanic majesty of Linosa and the tranquil solitude of Lampione, these islands offer a mosaic of experiences that beckon the soul to delve deeper, explore further, and embrace the serene complexity of island life.

As we set sail on this narrative journey, we are not merely traversing geographic distances; we are traversing chapters of a story that has been unfolding for millennia, a story that invites us to become a part of its unfolding mystery. Welcome to the Pelagie Islands, where every path leads to discovery, and every moment is a brushstroke on the canvas of the Mediterranean dream.

Another hidden treasure within the Pelagie Islands is the enchanting island of Linosa, a testament to the preservation of tradition. This small volcanic island, with its dramatic landscapes of black lava rocks and fertile soils, is home to a tight-knit community that deeply cherishes its age-old customs. The island's vibrant birdlife, including migrating species, adds to its ecological allure, making it a haven for nature enthusiasts and birdwatchers.

One of the highlights of island life is the Feast of San Giuseppe, a celebration that unites the locals through music, dance, and culinary delights, fostering a profound sense of community. The rugged beauty of Linosa, with its dramatic coastline, emerald green waters, and vibrant marine life, further enhances its charm, creating a paradise where culture and nature coexist in harmony.

For those seeking tranquility and untouched natural beauty, the uninhabited island of Lampione, a small rocky outcrop topped with a solitary lighthouse, offers a serene sanctuary. This island, part of a marine nature reserve, boasts pristine landscapes and untouched beaches, providing a peaceful haven for nature lovers and an exceptional spot for diving enthusiasts to explore the rich underwater biodiversity.

A journey through the Pelagie Islands is not just a mere trip, but an enriching cultural and historical exploration. From the dynamic and multicultural ambiance of Lampedusa, with its blend of Sicilian and North African influences, to the traditional and unspoiled beauty of Linosa, and the tranquil serenity of Lampione, these islands weave a unique narrative. Each island presents a chapter of a captivating story, inviting visitors to immerse themselves in a spectrum of cultural richness and natural splendor.

In Lampedusa, visitors are greeted with a mosaic of experiences – from the idyllic Spiaggia dei Conigli, known for its crystal-clear waters and soft sandy beaches, to the lively local scene offering fresh seafood delights and a glimpse into the vibrant island life. The island's importance as a nesting site for loggerhead turtles adds an ecological dimension to its allure.

The Pelagie Islands, with their combination of vibrant culture, deep-rooted traditions, and breathtaking natural beauty, offer an unforgettable experience that resonates with the essence of Italian charm. They stand as a beacon of Mediterranean allure, each island a unique jewel in the azure sea, beckoning travelers to discover their hidden wonders and leave with memories that will last a lifetime.

Chapter 6: Unique Italian Experiences

6.1 Wine and Gastronomy Adventures

In this section, there may be repetitions of topics, places, or sites that we have already discussed earlier in the book. However, we thought it would be useful to reiterate them in a dedicated chapter of this volume.

Italy, a land synonymous with culinary mastery and a rich wine heritage, stands as an enchanting paradise for food and wine enthusiasts. This country offers a tapestry of unique experiences that tantalize the taste buds and etch lasting impressions on the palate. Imagine yourself journeying through the rolling vineyards of Tuscany, each grape-laden vine telling a story of tradition and passion. Here, among the undulating hills, you'll find a plethora of wineries that beckon with the promise of exquisite tastings.

Embark on a sensory adventure as you traverse these vineyards, partaking in wine tasting tours that blend scenic beauty with the elegance of world-class wines. Knowledgeable sommeliers serve not only as guides through the rich flavors of each bottle but also as storytellers, weaving narratives of the winemaking process that echo the dedication and expertise of generations.

Beyond the vineyards, the heart of Italy's culinary genius beats in its diverse range of dining experiences. From the quaint, family-run trattorias nestled in the cobblestone streets of rustic villages to the opulent ambiance of Michelin-starred restaurants, every meal is a celebration of Italy's gastronomic prowess. Indulge in traditional dishes, each a symphony of flavors crafted from locally sourced ingredients and secret family recipes, whispered down through time.

Your gastronomic journey would be incomplete without a visit to Italy's vibrant food markets. The Mercato Centrale in Florence and the Mercato di Porta Palazzo in Turin stand as bustling epicenters of Italian cuisine. Here, amidst the colorful stalls, you'll discover a cornucopia of fresh produce, artisanal cheeses, expertly cured meats, and sinfully delectable pastries. Each market visit is an exploration of Italy's rich agricultural tapestry, a vibrant celebration of the country's deep connection to the land.

And then, there's the Italian gelato - a creamy confection that's a testament to Italy's love affair with desserts. From classic favorites to innovative creations, each flavor is a masterpiece, capturing the essence of Italian indulgence. Let every spoonful of gelato be a journey in itself, as you uncover the depth and variety of this beloved treat.

As you delve into the wine and gastronomy adventures across Italy, immerse yourself in the leisurely Italian lifestyle. Embrace each moment, letting the flavors of Italy dance upon your palate, and the stories behind each dish and wine fill your soul with joy. Italy is not just a destination; it's an experience, a celebration of the artistry of food and wine, wrapped in the warmth of Italian hospitality.

Your adventure begins in the sun-kissed vineyards of Tuscany and leads you through the charming wineries of Piedmont, each stop a chapter in Italy's rich enological narrative. As you journey, let Italy's culinary and vinous treasures unfold before you, creating a mosaic of experiences that are not just meals and tastings, but memories to cherish for a lifetime.

6.2 Unconventional Beach Escapes

Italy's coastline is a mosaic of breathtaking beach destinations, often overshadowed by the fame of the Amalfi Coast or the sun-kissed shores of Sicily. Yet, for those seeking a beach escape with a twist of the unconventional, Italy's lesser-known gems beckon with allure and mystery.

Nestled off the coast of Tuscany, the island of Elba emerges as a hidden treasure. Here, stunning beaches with crystal-clear turquoise waters offer a serene retreat from the world. Elba is a tapestry of diverse coastal landscapes, where secluded coves whisper secrets of tranquility and expansive sandy stretches echo with the gentle rhythm of the waves. This island isn't just a destination; it's a haven where the serene atmosphere and unspoiled beauty converge, creating a paradise for beach lovers and solitude seekers alike.

Venture into the heart of the Tyrrhenian Sea, and you'll discover Ponza, an island sculpted by nature's artistry. Known for its rugged coastline that cradles hidden grottoes and vibrant blue waters, Ponza is a canvas where the sea paints different shades of azure and cerulean. It's an underwater paradise for snorkelers and divers, offering a kaleidoscope of marine life. Exploring Ponza's underwater realms is like stepping into another world, one where the beauty and diversity of Italy's coastal ecosystems are on full display.

For an experience that's truly off the beaten path, the Tremiti Islands in the Adriatic Sea await. These small, yet majestic islands offer a tranquil escape where pristine beaches meld seamlessly with breathtaking views. Stroll along their soft sands, take a dip in the invigorating sea, or bask in the stunning coastal landscapes. The Tremiti Islands are not just a destination; they're a sanctuary where relaxation and rejuvenation are as boundless as the horizons.

Italy's unconventional beach escapes are not merely alternatives to the popular; they're invitations to explore the hidden jewels of the Italian coastline. These destinations offer a chance to immerse yourself in unspoiled natural beauty, embrace tranquility, and create memories that resonate with the soul's desire for discovery and adventure. From Elba's tranquil shores to Ponza's underwater wonders, and the idyllic serenity of the Tremiti Islands, each of these locales promises an experience that transcends the ordinary, leaving an indelible mark on your heart.

6.3 Hiking and Nature Trails

Italy, a country draped in natural splendor, offers a mosaic of hiking and nature trails that weave through its varied landscapes. From the majestic peaks of the Dolomites in the north to the untamed beauty of the Calabrian mountains in the south, the country is a paradise for outdoor enthusiasts seeking an immersive experience in nature.

The Dolomites, with their towering cliffs and verdant valleys, present a dramatic backdrop for adventurers. Here, trails meander through alpine meadows, past shimmering lakes, and beneath soaring limestone spires. Each path in the Dolomites tells a story, a narrative of the earth's power and beauty.

Venturing south, the Apennine Mountains form Italy's rugged backbone, offering a tapestry of trails that cater to every level of hiker. As you traverse these paths, you'll be greeted by ancient forests that whisper tales of the past, charming villages that showcase Italy's rich cultural heritage, and vistas that stretch to the horizon, offering breathtaking views that capture the essence of the Italian landscape.

Along the Amalfi Coast, the Sentiero degli Dei (Path of the Gods) awaits. This celestial trail offers hikers a heavenly perspective of the Mediterranean, with panoramic coastal views that are simply divine. The trail is not just a path but a journey through the clouds, where the sea and sky meet in a horizon of azure.

In the UNESCO-listed Cinque Terre National Park, a network of trails connects five iconic coastal villages. Each step along these paths brings you closer to the heart of Italian coastal life, with its vibrant colors, rustic charm, and the rhythmic sound of waves crashing against the cliffs. Here, the trails offer more than just a walk; they are a journey through living postcards, brimming with the spirit of the Riviera.

For those seeking an experience marked by the raw power of nature, the

Aeolian Islands, off Sicily's coast, are a geological wonder. Volcanic landscapes create a dramatic setting for trails that ascend to craters and descend to the sea. These islands are not just landmasses; they are natural sculptures carved by the elements, offering hikers breathtaking views of the Mediterranean's deep blue expanse.

Embarking on a hiking or nature trail in Italy is not merely a physical journey; it's a spiritual odyssey into the heart of the country's natural grandeur. It's an opportunity to step away from the pulsating rhythm of the cities and immerse yourself in the tranquility and rejuvenation that only nature can provide. In Italy, each trail is a path to discovery, a chance to forge a deep connection with the earth and to experience the serene beauty of the Italian landscape in its purest form.

6.4 Historical and Architectural Marvels

Italy, a country steeped in history, stands as an open-air museum showcasing a rich tapestry of historical and architectural marvels. From the sunbaked ruins of ancient civilizations to the soaring cathedrals that pierce the skyline, each region of Italy offers a unique journey through time and creativity.

In the heart of Rome, the Colosseum stands as a colossal testament to the might and ingenuity of the Roman Empire. This ancient amphitheater, a marvel of engineering and architecture, echoes with the tales of gladiatorial contests and grand spectacles. It is not merely a structure but a symbol of an era when emperors and citizens alike basked in the glory of Rome.

Nearby, the Pantheon, with its grand dome and ethereal oculus, continues to marvel visitors with its timeless beauty and architectural brilliance. The temple's design, harmonizing geometry and light, creates an almost celestial experience, reminding us of Rome's enduring legacy in architectural mastery.

Journeying northward to Florence, the city's skyline is dominated by the awe-inspiring Duomo. Officially known as Santa Maria del Fiore, this cathedral is a symphony of art and architecture. The red-tiled dome, an engineering feat of its time, and the intricate marble façade are testaments to the city's golden age of art and innovation. The Duomo is not just a church; it's a landmark of human achievement.

In the same city, the Ponte Vecchio arches gracefully over the Arno River.

This medieval stone bridge, adorned with shops and bustling with life, offers a picturesque stroll through history. The bridge's enduring charm lies in its blend of functionality and beauty, a hallmark of Florentine design.

Venice, the enchanting city of canals, is home to the resplendent St. Mark's Basilica. This architectural jewel, blending Byzantine and Venetian styles, dazzles with its gold mosaics and opulent artistry. The basilica, more than a religious site, is a canvas that narrates Venice's storied past.

Adjacent to the basilica, the Doge's Palace stands as a masterpiece of Gothic architecture. Once the heart of Venetian power, the palace's ornate façade and lavish interiors reflect the city's former glory and affluence. Each hall and corridor within the palace tells a story of politics, art, and intrigue.

In the sun-drenched lands of Sicily, the Valley of the Temples in Agrigento transports visitors to the era of ancient Greece. Walking amongst these majestic ruins, including the Temple of Concordia and the Temple of Hercules, one is enveloped in the grandeur of a civilization that shaped the Western world. These temples are not just stone structures; they are echoes of ancient voices and a legacy etched in marble and time.

Italy's historical and architectural marvels are endless, each region revealing its own chapter of the past. From Rome's imperial grandeur to Florence's artistic splendor, and from Venice's aquatic elegance to Sicily's ancient echoes, Italy is a mosaic of histories interwoven with art and architecture. These marvels await travelers who wish to delve deep into the heart of Italian culture, uncovering stories and wonders that span centuries.

6.5 Art and Culture Immersion

Italy, a country steeped in a rich tapestry of art and culture, presents endless opportunities for exploration and discovery. This land, where history and modernity intertwine, offers a myriad of experiences for those seeking to immerse themselves in its artistic and cultural heritage.

Venturing beyond the grand museums and renowned galleries, the true heart of Italian artistry beats in its small towns and villages. These locales are sanctuaries of traditional craftsmanship, where local artisans and craftsmen bring age-old techniques to life. Imagine the mesmerizing dance of a master glassblower in Murano, as they shape molten glass into intricate designs, or the careful precision of a ceramist in Deruta, crafting delicate pottery with patterns that tell stories of the past. These intimate experiences provide a window into the soul of Italian craftsmanship, showcasing the dedication and skill embedded in each unique creation.

In Italy's vibrant cities, art is not confined to the walls of galleries but spills onto the streets, creating a dynamic tapestry of creativity. Florence, the cradle of the Renaissance, boasts timeless masterpieces, while Milan's contemporary art scene pulsates with innovation and modern expression. Every corner of these cities offers a visual feast, from the classical sculptures that adorn public spaces to the bold street art that challenges and captivates.

The essence of Italian culture is perhaps best experienced through its myriad of festivals and events. The Carnival of Venice, with its opulent masks and theatrical performances, is a spectacle of historical grandeur. Meanwhile, the opera performances in Verona's ancient Roman arena are not mere shows but a journey through time and emotion, set against a backdrop of architectural splendor. These events are more than just celebrations; they are vibrant expressions of Italy's rich artistic legacy, offering a chance to engage with locals and immerse oneself in the authentic rhythm of Italian life.

From the serene ambiance of a rural artisan's workshop to the electric energy of urban art districts, and from the grandeur of historical festivals to the intimate corners of village squares, Italy beckons those who wish to delve deep into its artistic soul. Whether you find yourself lost in the masterpieces of Florence's Uffizi Gallery or sipping espresso in a quaint piazza, each moment spent in Italy is an opportunity to immerse yourself in an unparalleled world of art and culture.

6.6 Enchanting Rural Villages

Italy, with its tapestry of picturesque rural villages, offers an enchanting escape into a world where history and tradition weave seamlessly into the fabric of daily life. Nestled among rolling hills and verdant valleys, these hidden gems stand as timeless testaments to Italy's rich heritage and a more serene way of living.

As you meander through these enchanting villages, each step is a journey into the heart of authentic Italian culture. The cobblestone streets, lined with a riot of vibrant flowers, lead through a labyrinth of beauty where every nook and cranny tells a tale of yesteryears. These villages, with their centuries-old stone houses, are not just structures; they are the keepers of stories, the guardians of a bygone era.

The architecture in these rural havens mirrors the history of the regions, each stone and beam imbued with tales and craftsmanship passed down through generations. Intricate details adorn the facades, and each village boasts unique features that highlight the diverse tapestry of Italy's past.

In these idyllic settings, time seems to pause, allowing a glimpse into a life that cherishes age-old traditions and customs. The daily life here is a rhythmic dance of simplicity and harmony with nature. From the bustling marketplaces, echoing with the chatter of local vendors, to the quaint family-run establishments, there's an inherent sense of community and connection to the land.

Surrounding these villages, the natural landscape unfolds in a panorama of breathtaking beauty. Lush hills roll into the horizon, speckled with vineyards and olive groves that paint a scene straight out of a masterpiece. The air is a symphony of scents – fresh herbs, blooming flowers, and the earthy aroma of the countryside. It's a sensory retreat that rejuvenates the soul and reconnects one with the simpler joys of nature.

Yet, the true essence of these rural villages lies in the warmth and hospitality of their people. Italians, known for their geniality, open their hearts and homes, sharing the richness of their culture with every visitor. Engaging with the locals, whether through a shared meal or a village festival, transforms every visit into a personal and intimate experience, transcending the bounds of tourism.

Embarking on a journey to Italy's rural villages is to discover the soul of the country. Beyond the allure of its bustling cities, these villages offer a tranquil haven, a place where time slows down, and life's pleasures are savored. They're not just destinations; they are portals to a world where the past and present coexist in harmony, leaving visitors with memories etched in the heart, forever capturing the essence of the Italian spirit.

6.7 Hidden Gems for Adventure Seekers

Italy is not only a country of historical landmarks and picturesque landscapes but also a haven for adventure seekers. Beyond the well-known tourist destinations, there are plenty of hidden gems that offer thrilling experiences for those seeking an adrenaline rush. Here are some lesser-known but incredible destinations in Italy that cater to the adventurous souls:

Valle d'Aosta

Tucked away in the northwestern part of Italy, Valle d'Aosta is a true paradise for outdoor enthusiasts. The region boasts towering mountains, including the iconic Matterhorn and Monte Rosa, which provide fantastic opportunities for hiking, mountaineering, and skiing. One cannot miss visiting the Gran Paradiso National Park, known for its stunning alpine scenery and diverse wildlife.

Grotte di Castellana

Located in the region of Puglia, the Grotte di Castellana is a mesmerizing cave system that stretches for kilometers underground. Exploring these caves is like stepping into a hidden world of stalactites, stalagmites, and unique rock formations. Guided tours take visitors through the intricate maze of tunnels and chambers, revealing the geological wonders that lie beneath the surface.

Via Ferrata delle Bocchette

For thrill-seekers with a head for heights, the Via Ferrata delle Bocchette in the Brenta Dolomites is an unforgettable adventure. This via ferrata, or iron path, is a network of steel cables, ladders, and footpaths that traverse the rugged cliffs of the Dolomites. It combines hiking and climbing, offering breathtaking views and a thrilling challenge for experienced mountaineers.

Gola del Furlo

Nestled in the Marche region, the Gola del Furlo is a hidden gem for nature lovers and outdoor enthusiasts. This picturesque gorge is home to the Furlo Pass, an ancient Roman road carved into the cliffs. Hiking trails wind through the lush vegetation, leading to panoramic viewpoints and the opportunity to spot local wildlife, including golden eagles and peregrine falcons.

EXPLORING ITALY'S HIDDEN GEMS

Isola d'Elba

Located off the coast of Tuscany, the island of Elba offers a mix of natural beauty and adventurous activities. With its crystal-clear waters and rugged coastline, it's a paradise for snorkeling, diving, and kayaking. Exploring the island's trails on foot or by bike is also a great way to discover hidden coves, ancient ruins, and breathtaking vistas.

The Appennino Tosco-Emiliano National Park

Straddling Tuscany and Emilia-Romagna, this park offers a variety of hiking trails through its richly diverse landscapes. The park is also home to abundant wildlife and provides opportunities for bird watching and nature photography.

Lago di Garda

Italy's largest lake is a popular destination for windsurfing, sailing, and kitesurfing, thanks to its favorable wind conditions. The surrounding area also boasts picturesque trails for mountain biking and hiking, with stunning views of the lake.

Alta Via 1

A renowned long-distance trek in the Italian Alps, this trail stretches through some of the most beautiful and unspoiled parts of the Dolomites. It's a challenging hike that rewards trekkers with incredible views and a sense of accomplishment.

Monte Etna, Sicily

For a truly unique adventure, hiking on the active volcano of Mount Etna is a memorable experience. The landscape here is starkly different, characterized by volcanic craters and lava flows, offering a glimpse into the raw power of nature.

These hidden gems in Italy provide unique and thrilling experiences for adventure seekers. Whether you're into hiking, caving, mountaineering, or water sports, there's something for everyone in this diverse and beautiful country. Step off the beaten path and uncover the lesser-known treasures that await you in Italy's hidden corners.

6.8 Unveiling Italy's Underground Treasures

Indeed, Italy's subterranean world is as captivating and diverse as its surface, offering unique glimpses into the past and presenting a side of Italian history that is often overlooked. Here's an expanded exploration of Italy's underground marvels:

Catacombs of Rome

These ancient burial grounds are a labyrinth of narrow tunnels and chambers, weaving a tale of early Christian life and rituals. The catacombs, including those of San Callisto and San Sebastiano, are adorned with early Christian art, providing a haunting yet profound insight into the beliefs and practices of ancient Romans.

Matera's Sassi

In Southern Italy, Matera's Sassi are a remarkable testament to human ingenuity and adaptability. These ancient cave dwellings, some of the oldest continuously inhabited settlements in history, offer an unparalleled journey through time. The cave churches and homes, dug into the soft tufa rock, narrate the story of a community that thrived in challenging conditions.

Naples Underground (Napoli Sotterranea)

Beneath the bustling streets of Naples lies a fascinating network of tunnels and passageways. This underground city, dating back to Greek and Roman times, includes remnants of ancient theaters and a complex aqueduct system. Exploring Napoli Sotterranea reveals the multifaceted history of Naples, from its Greek origins to its development during Roman times and use as air raid shelters during World War II.

The Caves of Castellana (Grotte di Castellana)

Located in Puglia, these stunning karst caves are a geological wonder. The tour through the caves reveals a magical world of stalactites, stalagmites, and incredible rock formations, with the breathtaking "White Cave" being the highlight, known as one of the most beautiful caves in the world.

Orvieto's Underground City

The medieval city of Orvieto in Umbria hides a complex underground network of caves, tunnels, and wells, including the famous Pozzo di San Patrizio, a historic well with a double helix design. This underground labyrinth, carved into tufa rock, has a history of over 3000 years and was used for various purposes, from pigeon breeding to olive oil storage.

Turin's Underground Tunnels

The city of Turin in Northern Italy also has its share of underground secrets. The subterranean passages beneath the city have served multiple purposes over the centuries, including as a means of escape for royals and as bomb shelters during wars.

Exploring these underground sites in Italy is not just an adventurous experience but also a journey into the lesser-known chapters of Italian history. Each site, with its unique story and atmosphere, offers a different perspective on the country's past, from ancient times to the present day. For those willing to delve beneath the surface, Italy's underground treasures provide an unforgettable exploration of history, culture, and natural beauty.

Chapter 7: Off-the-Beaten-Path Experiences

7.1 Immersing in Local Festivals and Traditions

In this section, there may be repetitions of topics, places, or sites that we have already discussed earlier in the book. However, we thought it would be useful to reiterate them in a dedicated chapter of this volume:

Exploring Italy through its local festivals and traditions provides an exceptional window into the country's vibrant cultural mosaic. Across every region, city, and quaint village, Italy unfolds its diverse legacy through a series of vivid, deeply ingrained celebrations. Here's a closer look at some of the intriguing local festivals and customs across Italy:

La Tomatina di Ivrea

The northern town of Ivrea hosts this distinctive festival where participants engage in a spirited orange-throwing battle. This event is a modern-day portrayal of a medieval conflict, offering a unique and thrilling experience.

Calcio Storico Fiorentino in Florence

This ancient version of football, blending elements of soccer, rugby, and wrestling, is played in traditional costumes. Occurring every June, it's a fascinating insight into the medieval history of Florence.

Infiorata

Celebrated in several towns, notably Genzano and Noto, this June festival transforms streets into vibrant floral tapestries, created entirely from flower petals, demonstrating exceptional communal creativity and spirit.

Festa della Madonna Bruna in Matera

Every 2nd of July, Matera honors its patron saint with a grandiose procession, featuring an elaborate papier-mâché float that is spectacularly destroyed, symbolizing renewal and rebirth.

L'Ardia di San Costantino in Sardinia

In honor of Emperor Constantine's victory, this annual July horse race in Sedilo showcases remarkable equestrian skill and devotion, offering an exhilarating spectacle.

Festa del Redentore in Venice

Commemorating the end of the 1576 plague, this festival in July is marked by stunning fireworks and a pontoon bridge linking Zattere to the Church of the Redentore on Giudecca island.

La Quintana in Ascoli Piceno

This medieval jousting event in August is a colorful display of historical costumes, parades, and competition, celebrating Ascoli Piceno's rich cultural heritage.

Sagra dell'Uva in Marino

Known for the miraculous transformation of water into wine, this grape festival near Rome in October features fountains flowing with wine, free for public enjoyment.

Engaging in these festivals is an extraordinary way to partake in the living heritage of Italy. Each celebration is not just an event; it's a manifestation of history, local identity, and communal pride, offering visitors a chance to meaningfully connect with the Italian people. These festivals are more than mere spectacles; they are portals to the soul of Italy, narrating stories of a land rich in history, beauty, and a fervent celebration of life.

7.2 Exploring Italy's Hidden Natural Wonders

Italy, a land renowned for its art, history, and cuisine, also harbors a secret world of natural splendors. Beyond its bustling cities and iconic monuments lies a realm of hidden natural wonders, each offering a unique escape into landscapes that capture the imagination and awaken the spirit of adventure. From the tranquil islands of Sardinia to the majestic peaks of the Apennines, Italy's lesser-known natural attractions beckon the intrepid explorer to venture off the beaten path.

Asinara National Park, Sardinia: Discover this isolated island sanctuary where nature reigns supreme. Here, amidst the pristine landscapes, you can observe a remarkable array of wildlife in a setting that feels worlds away from civilization. The park is a haven for those seeking a genuine connection with the wild, offering unforgettable excursions into its untouched beauty.

Orrido di Botri, Tuscany: Venture into this dramatic gorge, a geological masterpiece carved by nature's hand. Hikers find themselves enchanted by the towering cliffs and the opportunity to spot the majestic golden eagle soaring above. It's a place where nature's grandeur is on full display, offering a rugged yet captivating adventure.

Lago di Braies, South Tyrol: Step into a fairytale at this enchanting alpine lake, renowned for its sparkling, crystal-clear waters and the breathtaking panorama of the Dolomites. Whether you're taking a serene boat ride or embarking on a lakeside hike, Lago di Braies is a destination that epitomizes the serene beauty of the Italian Alps.

Parco Nazionale d'Abruzzo, Lazio e Molise: Immerse yourself in this biodiverse sanctuary, home to some of Europe's rarest wildlife, including the elusive Marsican bear and the Apennine wolf. This park is not just a nature reserve; it's a living testament to Italy's commitment to preserving its natural heritage.

Parco Nazionale delle Foreste Casentinesi, Emilia-Romagna and Tuscany: Explore the ancient heart of Italy in this forested haven. It's a place where time seems to stand still, and the air is filled with the scent of old-growth trees and the sounds of nature's unspoiled beauty.Lago di Carezza, Trentino-Alto Adige: Behold the mystical beauty of this alpine lake, shrouded in legends and known for its striking emerald hues. Surrounded by forests and mountains, Lago di Carezza is a magical spot that captivates photographers and nature lovers alike.

Monte Sibillini National Park, Central Apennines: Traverse the breathtaking landscapes of this park, with trails leading through flower-filled plains and rugged peaks. It's a region rich in folklore and natural beauty, offering hikers a journey through some of Italy's most spectacular scenery.

Parco Nazionale del Gennargentu, Sardinia: Experience the wild heart of Sardinia in this diverse mountainous terrain. Here, hikers and nature enthusiasts can explore a landscape that ranges from high peaks to deep gorges, discovering the island's unique flora and fauna.

Riserva Naturale dello Zingaro, Sicily: Uncover the untouched beauty of Sicily's first nature reserve. Its pristine beaches and scenic hiking trails provide a peaceful retreat from the world, with stunning views of the Mediterranean Sea.

Lago di Sorapis, Veneto: Journey to this mesmerizing lake, famed for its distinctive turquoise waters. The hike through the Dolomites to reach this hidden gem is as rewarding as the destination itself, offering an adventure that is both challenging and awe-inspiring.

Le Dune di Piscinas, Sardinia: Wander through one of Europe's largest sand dune systems on the Sardinian coast. This desert-like landscape presents a stark contrast to the typical Italian countryside, offering a unique and surreal experience.

Monte Cofano, Sicily: Discover the rugged beauty of this coastal nature reserve. Its trails lead to panoramic views of the Sicilian coast, providing a perfect blend of sea, sky, and land.

Parco Naturale Adamello Brenta, Trentino: Delve into a world of alpine wonder in this expansive park. Known for its glaciers and tranquil lakes, the park is also a refuge for the brown bear, adding an element of excitement to every visit.

Valle dei Templi, Sicily: Experience the harmony of nature and history at this archaeological site, where ancient Greek temples stand amid a landscape of almond and olive trees. It's a place where the past meets the present in a serene natural setting.

Lago di Fusine, Friuli Venezia Giulia: Find tranquility at these twin alpine lakes, set against the backdrop of the Julian Alps. The peaceful environment is perfect for reflective strolls and soaking in the natural beauty of the region.

Parco Nazionale del Gran Sasso e Monti della Laga, Abruzzo: Explore one of Italy's largest national parks, a land of diverse landscapes from high mountain peaks to lush valleys. The park's rich biodiversity and stunning views make it a must-visit for nature enthusiasts.

Parco Nazionale del Cilento e Vallo di Diano, Campania: Discover the diverse beauty of this park, where mountains meet the sea. Along with its natural wonders, the park is steeped in history, offering a blend of outdoor adventure and cultural exploration.

Parco Nazionale dell'Arcipelago di La Maddalena, Sardinia: Sail through this archipelago's crystal-clear waters, exploring its islands and islets. Each island offers unique landscapes, from rugged coastlines to serene beaches, making it a paradise for water sports enthusiasts.

Parco Nazionale della Sila, Calabria: Venture into the heart of Calabria in this mountainous park. Its pine forests and artificial lakes create a serene environment, home to a variety of wildlife including the wolf, adding a sense of wilderness to every visit.

"Exploring Italy's Hidden Natural Wonders" invites you on an unforgettable journey through Italy's lesser-known but equally magnificent natural landscapes. Each destination offers a unique opportunity to connect with nature, delve into Italy's diverse ecosystems, and experience the serene beauty that lies hidden in this remarkable country.

7.3 Uncovering Italy's Lesser-Known Archaeological Sites

Italy, a country celebrated for its rich tapestry of history, is renowned not just for its well-known archaeological marvels like the Colosseum in Rome but also for its multitude of hidden historical treasures. Beyond the famous landmarks, Italy is dotted with numerous lesser-known yet equally fascinating archaeological sites, offering an off-the-beaten-path experience for travelers keen on delving into the country's vast cultural heritage. From the tranquil countrysides boasting ancient ruins to the lesser-trodden islands rich in historical remnants, Italy invites eager explorers to uncover its hidden gems.

Herculaneum, Campania: Just a short journey from the more crowded Pompeii lies the ancient city of Herculaneum. This well-preserved Roman town, also engulfed by the eruption of Mount Vesuvius in 79 AD, presents a different facet of ancient Roman life. Herculaneum, once a prosperous town, offers a glimpse into the luxurious lifestyle of its former inhabitants with its stunning villas, intricate mosaics, and the remains of an ancient boat, providing an intimate and immersive experience into the past.

Paestum, Campania: Venture further south to the archaeological park of Paestum, where the echoes of ancient Greek civilization resonate through its remarkable structures. Founded in the 6th century BC, Paestum is home to three beautifully preserved Greek temples – the Temple of Hera, the Temple of Neptune, and the Temple of Ceres. These structures, set against a backdrop of lush countryside, are a testament to the architectural prowess of the Greeks. The site also features Roman ruins, including a forum and an amphitheater, allowing visitors to traverse through different historical eras.

Ostia Antica, Lazio: Near Rome, the ancient port city of Ostia Antica offers an extraordinary journey back in time. Once a bustling commercial center, its well-preserved streets, houses, and public baths provide an authentic glimpse into the daily life of ancient Romans.

The Etruscan Tombs of Tarquinia, Lazio: Experience the mystique of the Etruscan civilization at Tarquinia. This UNESCO-listed site, with its intricately decorated tombs, offers a unique insight into one of Italy's earliest societies.

Valley of the Temples, Agrigento, Sicily: Journey to Sicily's Valley of the Temples, a breathtaking UNESCO World Heritage Site. Here, the ruins of ancient Greek temples, some of the best-preserved outside of Greece, stand majestically, telling tales of the island's ancient past.

Nora, Sardinia: On the picturesque southern coast of Sardinia, the archaeological site of Nora tells the story of Phoenician and Roman times. Its ruins include Phoenician walls, Roman baths, and a theater, complemented by the stunning coastal backdrop.

Roselle, Tuscany: Delve into the layered history of Roselle, where Etruscan and Roman ruins coexist, offering a glimpse into the transition of powers in ancient Italy.

Velia, Campania: In Velia, uncover the remnants of an ancient Greek and Roman city, revealing insights into the urban development and architecture of past civilizations.

Su Nuraxi di Barumini, Sardinia: Explore the unique Nuragic civilization at this UNESCO site. The central tower and surrounding village structures provide an understanding of prehistoric life on the island.

Fiesole, Tuscany: Overlooking the Renaissance city of Florence, Fiesole offers a blend of Etruscan and Roman ruins, set against the stunning Tuscan landscape.

Segesta, Sicily: In Sicily, the ancient city of Segesta showcases an unfinished Doric temple and an ancient theater, set amidst a landscape of rolling hills.

Aquileia, Friuli Venezia Giulia: This once-prominent Roman city captivates with its stunning ancient mosaics, offering a glimpse into the artistic endeavors of ancient Romans.

Antica Carsulae, Umbria: Walk the ancient Via Flaminia in Carsulae to discover a Roman city frozen in time, with its forum, theater, and arches narrating stories of its past.

Canosa di Puglia, Puglia: Rich in history, Canosa offers an array of tombs and artifacts that highlight the city's significance in ancient times.

Sepino, Molise: The remains of Samnite and Roman settlements in Sepino provide a unique look at the evolution of urban development in ancient Italy.

Pirgi e il Tempio di Giunone, Lazio: Discover the ancient Etruscan and Roman ruins at Pirgi, including the remarkable temple dedicated to Juno.

Parco Nazionale dell'Arcipelago di La Maddalena, Sardinia: Not just a natural wonder, this marine park is home to archaeological sites that tell the tale of the island's diverse historical influences.

Parco Nazionale della Sila, Calabria: Beyond its natural landscapes, Sila reveals remnants of ancient civilizations, adding a historical dimension to its natural beauty.

These lesser-known archaeological sites provide a unique opportunity to delve into Italy's rich and multi-layered history. They offer a tranquil exploration away from the crowds, allowing visitors to connect more intimately with Italy's past. For history enthusiasts and curious travelers, these hidden treasures of Italy are not just sites to visit; they are portals to a bygone era, each with its own story and ambiance, waiting to be uncovered and appreciated.

7.4 Delving into Italy's Artistic Hidden Gems

Italy is renowned for its rich artistic heritage, with world-famous museums and iconic landmarks attracting millions of visitors each year. However, beyond the well-trodden path, lie hidden artistic gems that offer a unique and authentic experience for art enthusiasts. Delving into Italy's artistic hidden gems allows you to discover lesser-known museums, galleries, and artistic treasures that are often overlooked by tourists. These hidden gems provide an opportunity to explore the lesser-known works of renowned Italian artists and gain a deeper understanding of Italy's artistic legacy. From small, quaint towns to secluded countryside villas, these off-the-beaten-path locations offer a refreshing alternative to the crowded art scenes in major cities.

Italy is renowned for its rich artistic heritage, with world-famous museums and iconic landmarks attracting millions of visitors each year. However, beyond the well-trodden path, lie hidden artistic gems that offer a unique and authentic experience for art enthusiasts. Delving into Italy's artistic hidden gems allows you to discover lesser-known museums, galleries, and artistic treasures that are often overlooked by tourists. These hidden gems provide an opportunity to explore the lesser-known works of renowned Italian artists and gain a deeper understanding of Italy's artistic legacy. From small, quaint towns to secluded countryside villas, these off-the-beaten-path locations offer a refreshing alternative to the crowded art scenes in major cities.

One such hidden gem is the Museo Diocesano in the charming town of Mantua. Nestled away from the bustling tourist crowds, this museum houses a remarkable collection of religious art spanning centuries. From exquisite Renaissance paintings to intricately carved sculptures, the Museo Diocesano showcases the lesser-known works of Italian masters such as Mantegna and Giulio Romano. Walking through the museum's hallowed halls, you can immerse yourself in the religious history and artistic brilliance of Italy.

For those seeking a tranquil retreat surrounded by artistic beauty, the Villa Cimbrone Gardens in Ravello is a hidden paradise. Tucked away on the Amalfi Coast, this secluded villa is adorned with stunning sculptures and breathtaking views of the Mediterranean Sea. As you wander through the meticulously manicured gardens, you will encounter hidden corners filled with ancient Roman statues and elegant marble fountains. The Villa Cimbrone Gardens provide a serene setting to appreciate the fusion of nature and art.

Another hidden gem worth exploring is the Pinacoteca Nazionale di Bologna. Located in the vibrant city of Bologna, this lesser-known museum houses a remarkable collection of Italian paintings from the Middle Ages to the 19th century. From the exquisite works of Giotto to the vibrant masterpieces of Morandi, the Pinacoteca Nazionale di Bologna offers a comprehensive journey through Italy's artistic evolution. The museum's intimate setting allows art enthusiasts to delve into the details of each painting and appreciate the nuances of Italian art.

Venturing off the beaten path in Italy not only allows you to escape the tourist crowds but also provides a deeper connection with the country's artistic heritage. These hidden gems offer a chance to explore the works of renowned Italian artists in a more intimate and personal setting. Whether you choose to visit the quaint town of Mantua, the serene Villa Cimbrone Gardens, or the vibrant city of Bologna, these off-the-beaten-path locations promise a truly unique and enriching artistic experience.

7.5 Discovering Hidden Culinary Delights

In the heart of Italy, a country celebrated for its profound culinary traditions, lies an adventure into tastes and flavors that transcends the well-known delights of pizza, pasta, and gelato. Exploring Italy's hidden culinary treasures offers a journey that is not only palate-pleasing but truly unforgettable. Italy's gastronomic landscape is a vivid tapestry, woven with regional specialties often overshadowed by its famous dishes but equally tantalizing.

Each corner of Italy boasts its distinct culinary identity, reflecting its unique history, geography, and culture. In the lush valleys of Piedmont, the hunt for aromatic truffles turns into a gastronomic quest. The region tempts visitors with dishes rich in earthy flavors, crowned by the prestigious white truffles of Alba. Similarly, Sicily's sun-kissed coasts yield a bounty of fresh seafood, each dish a celebration of the Mediterranean's generous offerings.

Venture off the beaten path to Emilia-Romagna, affectionately known as Italy's "Food Valley." This region is a treasure trove of culinary masterpieces such as Parmigiano Reggiano cheese, Prosciutto di Parma, and balsamic vinegar, all rooted in centuries-old traditions. The charming towns of Parma, Modena, and Bologna are not just stops on a map; they are sanctuaries of taste where every meal is a historical and cultural immersion.

In the south, Puglia's culinary charm lies in its simplicity and devotion to local ingredients. This sun-drenched region invites you to savor its signature orecchiette pasta with turnip greens, succulent seafood stews, and the creamy delight of burrata cheese. Dining in Puglia is a rustic experience, often in masserie or coastal trattorias, where the ambiance enhances the authenticity of each dish.

Heading north, Lombardy melds Italian and Alpine culinary influences, particularly in Milan, a city of fashion and gastronomic wonders. Here, traditional dishes like risotto alla Milanese and ossobuco tell stories of Lombardy's rich culinary heritage. The region also prides itself on its buttery pastries and Franciacorta, a sparkling wine that rivals the best champagnes.

Discovering Italy's culinary delights requires an immersive approach. Seek out family-run trattorias where generations-old recipes are lovingly prepared. These hidden gems, often tucked away in quaint streets or rural landscapes, are where the true heart of Italian cuisine beats the strongest. Here, every dish is prepared with passion, each recipe a legacy, and dining becomes an intimate connection with Italian culture and history.

From the truffle-laden tables of Piedmont to the sun-kissed seafood feasts of Sicily, from the rich culinary tapestry of Emilia-Romagna to the rustic, heartwarming meals of Puglia, and the sophisticated flavors of Lombardy, Italy promises a culinary journey like no other. Each region, each dish, is a chapter in Italy's grand gastronomic story, inviting you to savor and celebrate the diversity and richness of its culinary heritage. Prepare to indulge in a feast for the senses, where every bite is a discovery, and every flavor tells the story of Italy's vibrant and enduring love affair with food.

7.6 Off-the-Beaten-Path Hiking Trails

When it comes to exploring Italy's hidden gems, hiking trails offer a wonderful opportunity to immerse yourself in the country's natural beauty while venturing off the beaten path. Italy is home to a vast network of trails that cater to all levels of hikers, from beginners to experienced adventurers. These lesser-known trails take you through breathtaking landscapes, secluded valleys, and charming villages that are often overlooked by mainstream tourism. One such trail is the Sentiero degli Dei (Path of the Gods) located in the Amalfi Coast region. This scenic trail winds its way along the picturesque coastline, offering stunning views of the azure waters of the Tyrrhenian Sea and the rugged cliffs that characterize the area. As you hike along the Path of the Gods, you'll encounter ancient ruins, fragrant lemon groves, and traditional Mediterranean vegetation. The trail is relatively easy to moderate, making it suitable for hikers of all skill levels. Heading north to the Dolomites, you'll find the Alta Via 1, a long-distance hiking trail that spans across the majestic mountain range. This trail is perfect for experienced hikers seeking a challenging adventure. The Alta Via 1 takes you through breathtaking alpine scenery, including jagged peaks, tranquil lakes, and verdant meadows. Along the way, you'll also come across cozy mountain huts where you can rest and refuel while immersing yourself in the unique culture of the Dolomites. For those looking to explore the lesser-known islands of Italy, the Aeolian Islands offer a plethora of off-the-beaten-path hiking trails. Take a ferry from Sicily and embark on an adventure through these volcanic archipelago islands. Each island boasts its own unique landscape and charm, from the fiery Stromboli with its active volcano to the tranquil Salina with its lush greenery. Hiking trails on the Aeolian Islands allow you to discover hidden coves, pristine beaches, and breathtaking viewpoints that offer panoramic vistas of the Mediterranean Sea. When venturing off-the-beaten-path on hiking trails in Italy, it's essential to be well-prepared. Make sure to pack appropriate hiking gear, including sturdy footwear, a map or GPS device, and plenty of water and snacks. It's also advisable to check weather conditions and trail conditions beforehand and inform someone of your hiking plans. By following these precautions, you can make the most of these lesser-known hiking trails and create unforgettable memories while exploring Italy's hidden gems.

7.7 Exploring Italy's Hidden Beaches

Italy, renowned for its stunning architecture, rich historical tapestry, and exquisite cuisine, also boasts some of the world's most breathtaking hidden beaches. These secluded coastal gems provide tranquil escapes from the bustling tourist hotspots, inviting visitors to bask in the untouched splendor of the Italian coastline. From the crystal-clear waters of Sardinia to the charming coves of Sicily, Italy's hidden beaches are a must-visit for any beach lover.

The pristine beauty of Italy's lesser-known beaches is unparalleled. Imagine stretches of soft, golden sands bordered by shimmering turquoise waters, creating serene oases that seem almost surreal. Each hidden beach, from the secluded bays of the Amalfi Coast to the tranquil shores of lesser-traveled islands, has its unique charm and allure.

Consider the serene beauty of Cala Goloritzé in Sardinia, with its towering cliffs and azure waters, accessible only by foot or sea, offering an exclusive retreat into nature. Or picture the enchanting Spiaggia dei Conigli in Lampedusa, where crystal-clear waters meet pristine sands, making it one of the most beautiful beaches in the world.

The tranquility and serenity of these hidden beaches set them apart from the more popular destinations. Here, you can find personal sanctuaries where the rhythmic waves and gentle sea breeze are your companions. These beaches offer a perfect blend of relaxation and immersion in nature, allowing visitors to unwind and reconnect with the environment.

But the allure of Italy's hidden beaches extends beyond relaxation. They are portals to the country's rich cultural history. Near these tranquil shores, remnants of ancient civilizations abound – from Roman ruins to Byzantine mosaics. Imagine wandering along a secluded beach in Calabria, like the Spiaggia di Scario, and discovering the ruins of an ancient Greek temple, or uncovering Etruscan relics along the sandy stretches of Tuscany's coastline.

For beach enthusiasts, Italy's hidden beaches are undiscovered treasures, each with its own story. From romantic retreats in hidden bays like Baia dei Turchi in Puglia to family adventures on unspoiled islands like the Aeolian Islands, these shores offer diverse experiences. The hidden beaches near the Cilento National Park in Campania provide rugged mountain backdrops, while the secluded beaches of the Po Delta in Veneto are a haven for birdwatchers and nature lovers.

As you embark on this journey to Italy's hidden beaches, embrace both discovery and relaxation. Be prepared to explore narrow coastal paths, interact with local fishermen, and savor regional seafood delicacies in quaint seaside taverns. These hidden beaches are not just destinations; they are experiences that tantalize the senses and soothe the soul. Each visit promises not only a dive into Italy's natural beauty but also an intimate encounter with its rich history.

In conclusion, Italy's hidden beaches offer more than just picturesque destinations; they are gateways to experiences that enrich the soul. From the secluded coves of Liguria to the hidden shores of Sardinia and the volcanic landscapes of the Aeolian Islands, each beach is a unique slice of Italian paradise, waiting to tell its story and offer an unforgettable experience. So, let your journey to Italy's secluded shores begin, where every hidden cove and shimmering stretch of sand is a discovery and a treasure in its own right.

7.8 Unique Shopping Experiences: Local Artisans and Boutiques

When you think of shopping in Italy, the experience transcends the allure of luxury brands and designer boutiques, leading you instead into the heart of its artisanal heritage. This journey uncovers the local artisans and hidden boutiques that truly offer one-of-a-kind experiences, allowing you to discover authentic Italian craftsmanship while supporting local businesses. From the handcrafted leather goods of Florence to the delicate Murano glass of Venice, each region of Italy has its own unique artisanal specialty.

In the historic city of Florence, the tradition of leatherwork is more than a trade; it's a legacy. Here, skilled artisans create handcrafted leather goods that are as durable as they are stylish. The local shops in Florence are not just retail spaces; they are galleries showcasing the art of leather, with each bag, belt, or accessory bearing the mark of generations of craftsmanship.

Venice, known for its enchanting canals and historical grandeur, is also the home of intricate Murano glass jewelry. The art of Murano glassmaking is a tradition steeped in history, dating back to the 13th century. As you explore Venice's boutiques, you are introduced to a kaleidoscope of glass jewelry, each piece reflecting the skill and artistry of the Murano glassmakers.

Beyond these renowned cities, Italy's diverse regions offer their own unique crafts and traditions. For instance:

Ceramica di Deruta, Umbria: Known for its vibrant ceramics, Deruta's artisanal pottery is a colorful embodiment of Italian craftsmanship.

Intarsio in Legno, Sorrento: Sorrento's wood inlay art tells stories through intricate designs and detailed craftsmanship.

Cestineria in Vimini, Castelsardo, Sardegna: The wicker baskets from Castelsardo are not just functional; they are woven works of art.

Coltelleria di Scarperia, Toscana: The knives from Scarperia are famed for their quality, blending functionality with traditional design.

Vetro di Altare, Liguria: Altare's glassmaking tradition offers unique and lesser-known styles compared to Murano.

Lavorazione del Rame, Montepulciano: The copperworks in Montepulciano, from utensils to art pieces, showcase the metal's versatility.

Lavorazione della Pietra di Lecce: The soft Lecce stone is transformed into intricate sculptures and architectural pieces.

Tessitura del Lino, Burano: Burano's linen weaving is as delicate as its famous lace, a testament to the island's rich textile tradition.

Oreficeria, Valenza: The goldsmiths in Valenza craft exquisite pieces, each a symbol of Italian luxury.

Falegnameria Tradizionale, Umbertide: In Umbertide, traditional woodwork techniques are used to create timeless furniture and decor.

Tessitura a Telaio, Bevagna: Bevagna's loom-woven textiles are a blend of historical techniques and modern design.

Scultura in Marmo, Carrara: Carrara's marble sculptures are a continuation of the legacy that began in the Roman era.

Fabbricazione della Carta, Amalfi: Amalfi's papermaking, dating back to the Middle Ages, produces some of the finest paper in the world.

Ceramica, Caltagirone, Sicilia: Caltagirone's ceramics, especially the vibrant "Teste di Moro," are iconic representations of Sicilian art.

Maschere Veneziane, Venezia: Venice's handcrafted masks are a colorful echo of the city's famous Carnival.

Filigrana, Campo Ligure: The delicate filigree work of Campo Ligure is a fine example of Italian metalworking.

Pizzo di Cantù, Lombardia: The intricate lacework of Cantù is a testament to the region's delicate textile art.

Falegnameria Tradizionale, Selva di Cadore: In Selva di Cadore, traditional woodworking crafts unique furniture and decor pieces.

Tappeti, Pisticci: The handwoven carpets of Pisticci are colorful representations of Basilicata's artistic heritage.

Lavorazione del Corallo, Trapani: Trapani's coral work combines the beauty of the sea with intricate designs.

Coltelli di Pattada, Sardegna: The knives from Pattada are renowned for their craftsmanship and unique Sardinian style.

As you embark on this shopping journey across Italy, remember that you're not just acquiring products; you're participating in a story that spans generations. Whether it's the Tuscan ceramics, the Ligurian glasswork, or the Sardinian basket weaving, each item you purchase is a piece of Italy's rich cultural heritage.

Exploring these local artisan shops allows you to bring home a unique piece of Italy's rich cultural tapestry while supporting the livelihoods of the skilled craftsmen and women who keep these traditional arts alive. This journey through Italy's artisanal landscape is not just about shopping; it's an immersion into the heart of Italian culture and history.

Chapter 8: Practical Tips and Recommendations

8.1 Transportation Options: Getting Around in Italy

Italy offers a variety of transportation options for travelers to explore its hidden gems. Whether you prefer the convenience of flying or the scenic routes of train travel, there are plenty of choices to suit your needs. Here are some practical tips and recommendations for getting around in Italy: 1. Air Travel: If you're short on time or want to cover long distances quickly, flying is a convenient option. Italy has several major airports, including Rome Fiumicino Airport, Milan Malpensa Airport, and Venice Marco Polo Airport, which are well-connected to both domestic and international destinations. Consider booking your flights in advance to secure the best deals and avoid last-minute hassles. 2. Train Travel: Italy's rail network is extensive and efficient, making trains a popular mode of transportation for both locals and tourists. Trenitalia is the national train operator and offers a comprehensive network that covers major cities and smaller towns. The high-speed trains, such as the Frecciarossa and Italo, are a great option for long-distance travel, offering comfort and speed. 3. Regional Trains: To reach the lesser-known treasures of Italy, consider taking regional trains. These trains connect smaller towns and provide an authentic experience of the Italian countryside. While they may be slower than high-speed trains, they offer picturesque views and a chance to immerse yourself in the local culture. Remember to check the train schedules in advance, as they may have limited frequency. 4. Public Transportation: Once you arrive at your destination, public transportation is an excellent way to get around. Major cities like Rome, Florence, and Milan have efficient metro systems, buses, and trams that cover the city and its outskirts. Purchasing a travel pass or card can save you money and provide unlimited access to public transportation during your stay. 5. Rental Cars: If you prefer the flexibility of driving and exploring at your own pace, renting a car is a viable option. However, it's important to note that driving in Italy can be challenging, especially in historic city centers with narrow streets. Additionally, parking can be limited and expensive in popular tourist areas. Consider renting a car for exploring rural areas and smaller towns where public transportation options may be limited. 6. Ferries and Boats: Italy's beautiful coastline and islands can be easily accessed by ferries and boats. From the stunning Amalfi Coast to the picturesque islands of Sicily and Sardinia, these water transport options offer breathtaking views and a unique perspective of Italy. Research the ferry schedules in advance and consider booking tickets online to secure your spot, especially during peak tourist seasons. 7. Walking and Cycling: Exploring Italy's hidden gems on foot or by bike can be a rewarding experience. Many cities and towns have pedestrian-friendly areas, allowing you to stroll through charming streets and discover hidden treasures at your own pace. Renting a bicycle is also a popular option, especially in cities like Florence and Lucca, which have well-maintained cycling paths. Remember to plan your transportation arrangements in advance and consider a combination of different modes of transport to make the most of your trip. Each option offers its own unique advantages, so choose the one that best suits your preferences and travel itinerary.

8.2 Accommodation: Choosing Unique and Authentic Stays

When it comes to accommodation in Italy, there are countless options to choose from. While traditional hotels and resorts can provide comfort and convenience, opting for unique and authentic stays can enhance your experience and allow you to truly immerse yourself in the local culture. From charming bed and breakfasts nestled in historic towns to rustic farmhouses surrounded by vineyards, Italy offers a wide range of accommodation choices that cater to different preferences and budgets. Here are some practical tips and recommendations to help you choose the perfect place to stay during your Italian adventure:

For those seeking a truly immersive experience, staying at a charming bed and breakfast can be an excellent choice. These cozy establishments are often family-run and offer a warm and personalized atmosphere. Nestled in historic towns, they provide an intimate glimpse into the local way of life. Wake up to the aroma of freshly brewed coffee and indulge in a traditional Italian breakfast before setting out to explore the nearby cobblestone streets and ancient ruins.

If you're looking for a more rustic and idyllic setting, consider staying at a farmhouse in the Italian countryside. Surrounded by rolling hills and vineyards, these traditional farmhouses offer a serene retreat from the bustling cities. Wake up to breathtaking views of the countryside and savor a homemade breakfast made with fresh local ingredients. Spend your days exploring the sprawling vineyards, enjoying wine tastings, or simply relaxing amidst the natural beauty of the Italian countryside.

When choosing the perfect place to stay during your Italian adventure, it's essential to consider your preferences and budget. Italy caters to a wide range of budgets, from budget-friendly accommodations to luxurious retreats. Research different options, read reviews, and compare prices to find the ideal accommodation that suits your needs.

Additionally, consider the location of your accommodation. Italy is a country rich in history and culture, and staying in a central location can make it easier to explore the nearby attractions and landmarks. However, if you prefer a quieter and more secluded experience, consider accommodations in smaller towns or countryside locations.

Lastly, don't be afraid to embrace the local culture and traditions during your stay. Engage with the locals, try traditional dishes, and participate in local activities and events. This will not only enhance your experience but also create lasting memories of your time in Italy.

Overall, Italy offers a plethora of accommodation choices that can cater to every traveler's preferences and budget. Whether you choose a charming bed and breakfast in a historic town or a rustic farmhouse in the countryside, immersing yourself in the local culture will undoubtedly make your Italian adventure truly unforgettable.

8.3 Dining Tips: Trying Local Cuisine

When exploring Italy's hidden gems, one of the most exciting experiences is undoubtedly trying the local cuisine. Italian food is renowned worldwide for its rich flavors, fresh ingredients, and traditional cooking techniques. To fully immerse yourself in the culinary delights of each region, here are some practical tips and recommendations: 1. Visit Local Markets: Start by exploring the local markets in each town or city you visit. These vibrant markets are not only great for buying fresh produce, but they also provide a unique opportunity to interact with locals and discover regional specialties. From colorful fruits and vegetables to artisanal cheeses and cured meats, the markets offer a true feast for the senses. 2. Embrace Regional Specialties: Each region in Italy has its own unique culinary specialties. Whether it's the risotto in Lombardy, the pizza in Naples, or the pasta dishes in Emilia-Romagna, be sure to indulge in the local delicacies. Don't be afraid to step out of your comfort zone and try dishes that may be unfamiliar to you. This is the perfect chance to expand your palate and discover new flavors. 3. Seek Authentic Trattorias: While Italy is known for its world-class restaurants, don't overlook the humble trattorias. These family-run eateries often serve traditional, homemade dishes that are bursting with flavor. Look for places where locals dine, as they are likely to offer the most authentic and delicious meals. Don't be surprised if you find yourself enjoying a simple yet unforgettable meal in a small trattoria tucked away in a charming alley. 4. Follow the Locals: When in doubt about where to eat, follow the locals. Italians take their food seriously, and they know the best spots in town. Observe where the locals go for their lunch or dinner and join them. Whether it's a bustling pizzeria or a cozy osteria, you can trust that the food will be excellent. Engaging in conversations with locals can also lead to valuable recommendations and insights. 5. Don't Rush: In Italy, meals are meant to be enjoyed and savored. Unlike fast-paced dining experiences in some countries, Italians prefer to take their time when eating. So, when dining out, embrace the leisurely pace. Allow yourself to fully appreciate each bite, engage in conversations, and soak up the ambiance of the restaurant. Remember, a true Italian dining experience is not just about the food; it's about the entire sensory journey. By following these dining tips and recommendations, you can truly immerse yourself in Italy's culinary traditions and uncover the hidden gems of local cuisine. From the bustling markets to the authentic trattorias, each meal will be a memorable experience that adds richness to your exploration of Italy's lesser-known treasures.

8.4 Language Essentials: Useful Phrases and Expressions

When traveling to Italy, gaining a basic understanding of the Italian language can significantly enrich your experience. While English is commonly spoken in tourist areas, knowing some Italian phrases not only facilitates smoother interactions with locals but also shows respect for their culture.

Greetings and Basic Phrases:

Buongiorno (Good morning) – A respectful greeting for mornings, ideal for starting conversations with locals or staff at your accommodation. *Buonasera* (Good evening) – Use this from late afternoon onwards, especially when entering restaurants or shops.

Buonanotte (Goodnight) – Perfect for ending your day or when leaving an evening gathering.

Ciao (Hello/Goodbye) – A casual and friendly greeting, suitable for informal situations.

Grazie (Thank you) – Always appreciated, whether in a restaurant, shop, or when someone assists you.

Prego (You're welcome) – Used in response to *grazie* or to invite someone to proceed, like when holding a door open.

Ordering Food and Drinks:

Vorrei un caffè, per favore (I would like a coffee, please) – Essential for enjoying Italy's famous coffee culture.

Mi scusi, il conto per favore (Excuse me, the bill please) – Useful in restaurants to request the check.

Posso avere il menù? (Can I have the menu?) – Start your dining experience by asking for the menu.

Mi piacerebbe assaggiare la pasta alla carbonara (I would like to try the pasta alla carbonara) – Show interest in local cuisine by expressing your desire to try specific dishes.

Asking for Directions:

Scusi, dov'è la stazione? (Excuse me, where is the train station?) – Essential for navigating Italy's extensive train network.

Come arrivo a...? (How do I get to...?) – Helpful when seeking directions to a specific location.

È lontano? (Is it far?) – Gauge the distance before deciding whether to walk or take transportation.

A sinistra/A destra (To the left/To the right) – Basic direction phrases that can guide you through Italy's charming streets.

Shopping and Bargaining:

Quanto costa? (How much does it cost?) – Understand the price before making a purchase, especially in markets.

È troppo caro (It's too expensive) – A phrase that can initiate bargaining in informal markets.

Posso avere uno sconto? (Can I have a discount?) – Don't hesitate to ask for a discount, it's often part of the shopping culture in local markets.

Mi piace molto, lo prendo (I really like it, I'll take it) – Use this phrase to confirm your purchase decision.

Emergency Phrases:

Aiuto! (Help!) – Important in urgent situations.

Ho perso il mio passaporto (I lost my passport) – Necessary if you find yourself in this unfortunate situation.

Mi sento male (I feel sick) – Useful if you need medical attention.

Chiamate la polizia (Call the police) – In case you need law enforcement assistance.

Remember, Italians generally respond warmly to anyone attempting to speak their language. Even a few basic phrases can open doors to richer interactions and deeper cultural immersion. So, don't be shy—embrace the opportunity to practice your Italian, and you'll find that it enhances your travel experience in beautiful Italy.

8.5 Safety Considerations for Off-the-Beaten-Path Travel

1. Research Your Destination

Before setting off on your off-the-beaten-path adventure in Italy, take the time to research and understand your destination. Familiarize yourself with the local customs, traditions, and any specific safety concerns. Look into the political stability of the region and check for any travel advisories or warnings issued by your country's embassy or consulate. This will help you make informed decisions and stay prepared.

2. Plan Your Itinerary Carefully

When exploring lesser-known areas of Italy, it is essential to plan your itinerary carefully. Identify the places you wish to visit and evaluate their accessibility, transportation options, and proximity to emergency services. Consider sharing your travel plans with a trusted friend or family member so they can stay informed about your whereabouts.

3. Stay Connected

Ensure you have a reliable means of communication while traveling off the beaten path. Carry a fully charged mobile phone with an international SIM card and save emergency contact numbers. Be aware that in some remote areas, network coverage may be limited, so it's advisable to carry a satellite phone or a portable Wi-Fi hotspot device.

4. Be Mindful of Your Belongings

While exploring lesser-known treasures, it's important to be mindful of your belongings. Keep your valuables secure and avoid displaying signs of wealth. Consider using a money belt or a concealed pouch to carry your passport, cash, and important documents. It's also recommended to make digital copies of your travel documents and store them securely online.

5. Blend In with the Locals

To enhance your safety, try to blend in with the local culture and dress modestly. Avoid drawing unnecessary attention to yourself as a tourist. Learn a few basic phrases in Italian to navigate through interactions and show respect for the local customs. Being mindful of your surroundings and adapting to the local norms can greatly contribute to a safe and immersive travel experience.

6. Trust Your Instincts

Always trust your instincts when traveling off the beaten path. If a situation or a place feels unsafe or uncomfortable, it's best to remove yourself from it. Pay attention to your gut feelings and be prepared to change your plans if necessary. Your safety should always be your top priority.

By following these practical tips and recommendations, you can ensure a safe and enjoyable journey while exploring the lesser-known gems of Italy. Remember, adventure and discovery can go hand in hand with responsible and cautious travel.

Chapter 9: Conclusion

9.1 Reflecting on the Hidden Gems Explored

Throughout this journey of exploring Italy's hidden gems, we have delved into the lesser-known treasures that this beautiful country has to offer. From the picturesque villages nestled in the rolling hills of Tuscany to the charming coastal towns along the Amalfi Coast, we have uncovered the hidden gems that often go unnoticed by tourists. It has been a truly eye-opening experience to discover the rich history, vibrant culture, and breathtaking landscapes that these hidden gems possess. These off-the-beaten-path destinations have provided a unique perspective on Italy, allowing us to escape the crowds and immerse ourselves in the authentic charm of each region. Reflecting on the hidden gems we have explored, we can't help but feel grateful for the opportunity to uncover these hidden treasures and share them with fellow travelers seeking a more intimate and genuine Italian experience.

9.2 Inspiring Future Adventures

As you come to the end of this book, I hope you feel inspired to embark on future adventures in Italy. This diverse country offers endless possibilities for exploration and discovery, and there are still so many hidden gems waiting to be unveiled. Whether you've already visited some of the famous destinations or you've focused on the lesser-known towns and islands, there is always more to see and experience in Italy. From the bustling streets of Rome to the picturesque vineyards of Tuscany, from the charming canals of Venice to the breathtaking cliffs of the Amalfi Coast, Italy never fails to captivate with its beauty and history. So, where will your next Italian adventure take you? Perhaps you'll venture off the beaten path to the enchanting region of Puglia, with its whitewashed trulli houses and stunning coastline. Or maybe you'll explore the rugged landscapes of Sardinia, dotted with ancient nuraghe and pristine beaches. The possibilities are truly endless, and each region has its own unique charm and attractions. Don't be afraid to step outside your comfort zone and discover the hidden treasures that Italy has to offer. Whether you're a history enthusiast, a nature lover, a foodie, or an art aficionado, Italy has something to offer everyone. So go ahead and start planning your next adventure. Buon viaggio!

9.3 Leaving a Positive Impact

When exploring Italy's hidden gems, it is important to leave a positive impact on the places you visit. Responsible and sustainable tourism practices not only help preserve the natural beauty and cultural heritage of these lesser-known treasures but also contribute to the local economy and community. Here are some practical tips to ensure you leave a positive footprint: 1. Respect the Environment: As you venture into Italy's lesser-known destinations, be mindful of the fragile ecosystems and natural habitats. Avoid littering, stick to designated trails, and follow any guidelines or restrictions in place to protect the environment. 2. Support Local Businesses: Instead of relying solely on large chain hotels and restaurants, seek out locally-owned accommodations, eateries, and shops. By supporting local businesses, you contribute directly to the local economy and help sustain the unique character of these hidden gems. 3. Engage with the Community: Take the time to interact with the locals and learn about their customs, traditions, and way of life. Engaging with the community not only enriches your travel experience but also fosters mutual understanding and respect. 4. Be Mindful of Cultural Heritage: Many of Italy's hidden gems boast rich historical and cultural heritage. Show respect for these treasures by following any preservation guidelines, refraining from touching or removing artifacts, and being aware of the historical significance of the places you visit. 5. Travel Responsibly: Consider the impact of your transportation choices on the environment. Whenever possible, opt for public transportation or eco-friendly modes of travel. Additionally, be mindful of your energy and water consumption, and try to minimize waste while staying in these lesser-known destinations. By adopting these practices, you can ensure that your exploration of Italy's hidden gems leaves a positive and lasting impact, both for the places you visit and for future travelers to come.

9.4 Final Thoughts

In conclusion, exploring Italy's hidden gems provides a unique and enriching travel experience that goes beyond the well-known tourist destinations. Throughout this book, we have delved into the lesser-known treasures of each region, uncovering their beauty, rich history, and cultural significance. By venturing off the beaten path, travelers can discover charming villages, breathtaking landscapes, and authentic local experiences that showcase the true essence of Italy. From the picturesque coastal towns of Liguria to the idyllic countryside of Umbria, Italy's hidden gems offer a glimpse into the country's diverse and captivating offerings. The exploration of lesser-known destinations also contributes to the dispersion of tourism, reducing overcrowding in popular areas and supporting local economies. By promoting sustainable and responsible travel, visitors can help preserve the unique charm and authenticity of these hidden gems for future generations to enjoy. So, whether you're a history enthusiast, a nature lover, or a foodie seeking culinary delights, Italy's hidden gems are waiting to be discovered and cherished.

We invite you to leave a positive review and share this guide with your friends. After using it on your next trip to Italy, we would appreciate your feedback on its usefulness. Your insights and experiences can help other travelers discover and enjoy Italy's hidden wonders, enriching their own adventures. Your contribution is invaluable in enhancing and refining future editions of this guide. Thank you for

choosing to explore Italy with us, and we look forward to hearing about your journey!

9.5 Copyright

Copyright © 2023 by Julio De Cesari

All rights reserved. No part of this publication may be reproduced, distributed, or transmitted in any form or by any means, including photocopying, recording, or other electronic or mechanical methods, without the prior written permission of the author, except in the case of brief quotations embodied in critical reviews and certain other noncommercial uses permitted by copyright law.

For permission requests, write to the author at the address below.

arliessefolliana@gmail.com

EXPLORING ITALY'S HIDDEN GEMS

First Edition 2023

Available exclusively at Amazon.com

Printed in the United States by Amazon Print on Demand

FROM THE AUTHOR

Dear Reader,

As we reach the final pages of "Exploring Italy's Hidden Gems," I want to take a moment to extend my heartfelt thanks to you. I hope this book has not only taken you on a journey through Italy's landscapes and cultures but also provided a rich and memorable experience, whether you traversed the Italian streets in reality or traveled comfortably from your armchair.

Italy is a country of extraordinary beauty and profound diversity, and my aim was to showcase its lesser-known corners and stories, which are no less fascinating. If these pages have helped you to know and appreciate Italy more deeply, to discover its off-the-beaten-path aspects rich in authenticity, then I have accomplished my goal.

Your feedback is invaluable to me. If you enjoyed the book, I would be grateful if you could take a moment to leave a review. Your words can guide other readers in their discovery of the less-traveled Italy. And, if for any reason, something did not meet your expectations, I invite you to write directly to our email. Every comment, every suggestion, is a step towards improvement.

Thank you for traveling with me through the pages of "Exploring Italy's Hidden Gems". I hope this book has kindled in you a curiosity to explore these enchanting places in person and to experience your own adventures in Italy.

With gratitude, Julio De Cesari

Printed in Great Britain
by Amazon